The Great and Wondrous Sign

(The Lion, The Virgin and The Great Red Dragon)

"The heavens declare the glory of God;
And the firmament shows His handiwork.
Day unto day utters speech,
And night unto night reveals knowledge.
There is no speech nor language
Where their voice is not heard.
Their line has gone out through all the
earth,
And their words to the end of the world."
Psalm 19:1-6

Inscription

To my two precious daughters
whom I love with all my heart,
Liriel and Shay,
and their love of books!

Special thanks

To my wonderful Mom,
Virginia Hyde,
who always listened to my many ideas
and believed in me;
I stand, here, and honor you.

Special thanks to the following:
Christine Giannoni at the Field Museum of Natural History, Chicago, Illinois, who went above and beyond to secure one-time permission to use the Dragon Rubbing by David Crockett Graham D.Sc., Ph.D., B.D., F.R.G.S.
Marilyn Shea, Ph.D., Professor of Psychology, University of Maine at Farmington, who allowed the use of her photograph of an artifact from China, The Azure Dragon - 苍龙 - Han Dynasty 206 BCE-220 CE
European Southern Observatory and Martin Kornmesser for the illustration of Antares.
Jeff Dahl and Sodacan, who are hard working Wikipedia artist-contributors for the Egyptian Crown illustrations and the Azure Dragon Flag illustration.
Marie-Lan Nguyen for her photograph of an historic gold ring artifact with the engraved portrait of Ptolemy VI Philometor, located in the Louvre, Paris France.
Johannes Hevelius, who in 1690, created a fantastic map of the constellations called, "Firmamentum Sobiescianum sive Uranographia".
Special thanks to Laurence Hayworth of Look and Learn Ltd., London England, who so generously licensed The Three Wise men painting by James E. McConnell.
And last but not least, a very special thank you to the many contributors to the Stellarium Developers, who gave generously of their time, passion and expertise to design and program a wonderful star charting computer program that allows everyone to access information on the stars for FREE! (Download it, I highly recommend it!)
(None of the people or institutions listed have endorsed the facts or opinions stated in this book.)

Prologue

My purpose

My purpose for this book is to glorify God. By clearly pointing to the event of the Great and Wondrous Sign, I hope to inform those who would glorify God with me over this fulfillment of prophecy.

It is not my intention to cause controversy or to side with one view of the End Times over another. I hope to address these issues with respect and fairness. I am very much trying to remain neutral and I ask of you, the reader, to please be patient and continue reading even if there are things you don't agree with. I have gone over and over this manuscript removing as much controversy as possible. The evidences I document in this book are compelling and fascinating, as well as essential for every Christian to be aware of. With that being said, if you're a skeptic, keep reading. This next section will lay the groundwork and provide as much evidence and perspective as possible. If you're not a skeptic, you might find this next section interesting, or you might skip to chapter 1.

My Goal   The goal for this book is to alert the Body of Christ, the Church, as well as those who will come to believe, to the coming of "Great and Wondrous Sign" written of in Revelation 12. The Great and Wondrous Sign is a sign in the Heavens. It is knowledge revealed in the stars and spoken of in scripture, thousands of years before it was to happen. This sign is no longer a mystery and because of technology, we can look into the future of the stars using star tracking computer programs and see exactly when this sign takes place.

I am not the only person to have discovered this event. When I discovered it, I searched the internet and found several others who have found the same thing, and more are discovering it all the time.

I am not infallible, but I am trusting in God
I do not claim to know the mind of God, nor can I limit Him, so I expect that while this research will most likely have to be revised as events play out, I do believe that God has told me by His word, "Open wide your mouth and I will fill it.", so in that sense, I am claiming that this message, about the Great and Wondrous Sign, is a word from the Lord, and as such, I have an immense responsibility to transmit it clearly and without injecting personal opinion. I will however, explain what I have discovered thoroughly, so as to be understood. The ability to interpret signs in the stars comes from God and He alone deserves all glory and honor and praise. My task has been to seek this knowledge from Him and it is my humble position to endure any ridicule that may arise from this message. I only ask that you hear me out before you decide to make a judgment. This is a very complex, multi-facetted subject, which, as befitting of God, is only able to be partially understood by our finite minds. So, come, let us reason together.

What the purpose of this book is NOT
Please listen to what I am about to say: the purpose of this book is not, I repeat not to set a day or an hour of Christ's Return. The reason Jesus said, "No one knows the day or hour, not the angels in Heaven, nor the Son, but only the Father." (Matt. 24:36)

is because God is in charge of that. Secondly, the stars and planets do not work like that and also, there is room left in scripture for Christ's return to take place within a window of time, which is up to God the Father.

Also, I would point to a distinction between what has become known as "The Rapture" and events known as the "Second Coming" and "The Day of the Lord". These have different names and I believe that is for a reason. Please, consider what I have to say, but I encourage you to feel comfortable in your current belief of when End Times events will play out.

Why the stars? The Bible establishes very early on, in Genesis 1:14, "God said, "Let there be lights in the Heavens which divide the day and night; and let them **be for signs**, **for seasons**, marking off day<u>s</u> and years." Because the word "days" there is plural, it implies groups of days, such as weeks, months or lunar cycles. More significantly, please take note that the verse says that God's expressed purpose for the lights in the Heavens are to "be for signs" and seasons. This book will explain in detail why and how the stars are involved in fulfilling the prophecy of Revelation Chapter 12.

One reason we cannot know a day or an hour is, when looking at the stars, one cannot say, "Okay, <u>now</u> the planet has moved out of such and such a constellation." This is because planets move much slower across the field of stars than to designate a day or an hour. Even the movement of a planet across an imaginary line could very well take longer than a day or an hour.

Most Christians rightly believe that we cannot know the day or the hour of Christ's return. I agree with that because that's exactly what the Bible says. But some go beyond the scripture when they say, "So then, we cannot know <u>anything</u> about when Jesus will return!" Is that really so? Doesn't the Bible say we can know the season of His return? Why? So we will not be caught unaware. Let's go to the Scripture and see what it has to say about that:

1 Thessalonians 4:15-5:4

"...and the dead in Christ will rise first. After that, we who are still alive and are left will be caught up in the clouds to meet the Lord in the air. And so we will be with the Lord forever. Therefore encourage one another with these words. Now, brothers, about times and dates we do not need to write to you, for you know very well that the day of the Lord will come like a thief in the night. While people are saying, "Peace and safety" destruction will come on them suddenly, as labor pains on a pregnant woman*, and they will not escape. <u>BUT YOU, BROTHERS ARE NOT IN DARKNESS THAT THIS DAY SHOULD SURPRISE YOU LIKE A THEIF.</u>"

Let's unpack that a little. First, as this passage relates to Revelation 12, it is very much talking about labor pains of a pregnant woman; because that is the analogy being depicted in the Great and Wondrous Sign which addresses the troubling times the world will face just before Christ sets up His Kingdom.

Secondly, this passage from Thessalonians says "But you, brothers are not in darkness that this day should surprise you like a thief." This clearly tells us that we will not be surprised by the coming of the Lord. Something will alert us, and I believe that "something" is the Scripture.

There are many prophetic signs to be watching for and the greatest of those signs is The Great and Wondrous Sign in Revelation chapter 12.

There are several terms used in the Bible referring to events of the end times. The event that has come to be known as "The Rapture" is when all Christians, both the dead who are raised to life, and those of us who are still alive are caught up in the clouds to meet the Lord in the air. Take special note of those words, "in the air". Christ does not return to the earth at that time. The other event known as "The Day of the Lord" begins when Christ's foot touches down on the Mount of Olives and He destroys the enemies of God and comes to the rescue of the Jewish people. The Bible warns us to keep watch, and be aware of the end times.

Luke 21:34 says, "Be careful, or your hearts will be weighed down with carousing, drunkenness and the anxieties of life, and that day will close on you like a trap." Other versions say, "catch you unawares", "or that day will catch you by surprise." We are told over and over to be watchful, and "when we see these things happening" to know His return is very close.

Mark 13:28-29 Jesus said, "Now learn this lesson from the fig tree: As soon as its twigs get tender and its leaves come out, you know that summer is near. Even so, when you see these things happening, you know that it [the return of Christ] is near, right at the door."

The Authority to govern the stars.

Isaiah 40:26

> "Lift up your eyes and look to the heavens: Who created all these? He who brings out the starry host one by one and calls forth each of them by name. Because of his great power and mighty strength, not one of them is missing."

Only God has authority to establish the courses of the planets, their interaction with constellations and the exact time of Christ's return. Human beings cannot say, "because I say so, this or that planet will do such and such." Not even the Angels in Heaven have this power, but only God. This authority is referenced when Jesus says, "But about that day or hour no one knows, not even the angels in heaven, nor the Son, but only the Father." Matthew 24:36

According to one of the most significant Jewish scholars of the medieval ages, Rabbi Moses ben Maimon (referred to as "Rambam" or "Maimonides"), the time at which the names of the constellations were chosen was during the time of the Great Flood. According to Josephus, the Jewish historian, Adam, Seth and Enoch (7th from Adam, Noah's Great Grandfather) preserved information about the constellations on pillars of stone.

The Great Flood reference by Rambam and the history of Josephus are linked by Enoch, who would have known both Adam, Seth and Noah. So the history of the stars and the meaning of the constellations is very ancient and has a basis in both history and the Bible.

Jer. 32:17 Ah Lord God! Behold, You have made the heavens and the Earth by Your great power and outstretched arm. There is nothing to hard for You."

The appearance of the Great and Wondrous Sign is similar to the way Jesus taught through parables and also how God teaches through historical accounts in the Old Testament. God, being the master author, uses grand themes, symbols and stories to illustrate very visually for us what He wants to convey.

As it says in Psalm 19:1-6, "There is no language or speech where their voice is not heard." These powerful ideas will be discussed at further length in this book, to help deepen our understanding of the Great and Wondrous Sign and what it is God is telling us through it.

Also, this book is NOT about "astrology". While I have reviewed a diverse sampling of information concerning the stars while researching Biblical prophecy, what I have discovered is, modern astrology has taken what God intended and turned into a system of fortunetelling and superstition, which serves only to confuse those who would seek a clearer understanding of what God intended the stars to say. King David wrote: "Day after day they pour forth speech, night after night they utter knowledge."

Most of the knowledge we need is found in "astronomy" (not astrology), or simply being familiar with the stars, the Sun, Moon and planets. What I am interested in is the original meaning of the constellations, as set forth by our Creator. The primary basis for this information is the Bible. It talks about the stars more than one might realize and establishes most of their intended meanings, which will be discussed in further detail.

When I refer to sources other than the Bible, I will first refer to sources the Bible refers to, such as the Magi, believed to be from the area of Babylon, who studied the stars accurately enough to predict the birth of Christ and navigate to where He was born, and any other sources will be the oldest possible archaeological references to the signs which the Bible mentions.

Persian and Arabian traditions credit Adam, Seth and Enoch with the invention of Astronomy. The Hebrew Historian Josephus says Seth and his offspring preserved ancient astronomical knowledge in pillars of stone.(Josephus, The Antiquities of the Jews, Book I:1–3.)

Because of historical evidences such as this, there are many who believe the constellations of the Jewish/Hebrew "Mazzaroth", and the names of the stars associated with them were originally created as a mnemonic device by Adam, Seth and Enoch to preserve the true history of the world, as well as to point prophetically to the promised Messiah.

Acknowledgements

I also would like to acknowledge a few of my forerunners, particularly Dr. D. James Kennedy, who delivered a wonderful message about the original meaning and purpose of the constellations. I drew inspiration from Lou Giglio and his presentations on the stars. But probably the biggest inspiration to my quest was Law Professor Rick Larson, creator of a DVD titled "The Star of Bethlehem". I have used similar star tracking software to track the stars that he did, and his quest to find God's design in the physical cosmos is foundational to this book.

About Bible translations used in this book

It is my sincere intention to be as inclusive of the entire Body of Christ, the Church, wherever she may be in the world because this message is for all of us. Some stand by one translation and say that it is the only valid one. That is not my call. If you prefer a certain translation, I encourage you, please use the translation you feel most comfortable with and look up the scripture for yourself. I would prefer everyone to do that, digging further into the Bible and allowing God to speak to them through His Word. However, because I will be dealing with specific passages and verses, and must communicate in writing about them, I will be using several translations.

I will be diligent to search out the most accurate Biblical information possible as it pertains to the stars.

My Story

A little bit about myself. I grew up in a Christian home. My Father held a degree in Bible from Multnomah Bible College in Portland, Oregon. My Mother attended Bible College as well and came from a family full of missionaries and pastors, most notably, her parents, Jim and Margaret Buerer spent 15 years in the Central Republic of Africa as missionaries, after having served faithfully in the pastorship while raising their seven children. We attended several churches as I grew up, and as a matter of reference, I think it's useful to say what denominations they were. From 0-7 years, the church I attended was an "American Sunday School Union", a non-denominational church where my father taught the high school Sunday school class. From 7-10, my family attended an "American Missionary Fellowship" church, where my father taught the adult Sunday school, served as a worship leader and taught a mid-week Bible Study.

My Father died when I was 10, in an auto accident and my Mom and I attended a GARB Baptist Church for a couple years. When she remarried, we moved and we attended a Conservative Baptist Church from 12-18 years of age.

Here, I'd like to mention Larry Glazner, the man who pastored our High School Youth Group. As he met with us every morning before school for Bible study and prayer, he taught us how to experience the presence of God (The Holy Spirit). During my high school years, I volunteered with Child Evangelism Fellowship, teaching 5-day clubs and counseling at summer Bible camps.

I also attended Summit Ministries, a two week worldview seminar in Colorado Springs.

When I left for college, I attended another Conservative Baptist Church where I taught Jr. High Youth Group, worked as a janitor and as a volunteer sound technician. I later attended a Nazarene Church for 6 years and then a Village Missions church for 8 years, in my young adult life. I received a degree from a community college and entered full time ministry working for a Christian radio station in Coos Bay Oregon, where I hosted my own music and devotional show for 6 and a half years. During this time, I listened to around 10,000 sermons from some of the best preachers in the USA, as I like to think this would be equivalent to a Bible degree or the number of sermons a person hears in 90 years going to church twice a week... I also spent 2 hours a day researching the Bible and preparing about 1700 devotional messages to be presented on the air. I then became self employed as a professional potter, owned a chocolate shop for several years and hosted several arts and crafts shows. I enjoy painting, song writing and composing on the guitar and piano.

My background in stars

I love the stars, but have only recently learned very much about them. As a 7th grader, I spent an entire summer sleeping on an old couch on the back porch of our family home so I could watch the stars, meteorites and satellites every night as I fell asleep. (There were only a few visible satellites per night back then, in 1987) I considered my knowledge about the stars to be pretty average and dreamt of someday becoming an astronaut, much like many other young kids growing up during the "space age".

Later, while working at the Christian radio station, I heard a broadcast by Dr. D. James Kennedy, talking about the original, God-given meaning of the constellations (as opposed to the occult beliefs in modern astrology or ancient mythological beliefs of the Greeks). Also, I heard a program on the radio about Bethlehem's Star and a man, Rick Larson, who had used a star tracking computer program to wind-back the stars to the time of Christ's birth, where he discovered the star of Bethlehem to be a set of conjunctions between Jupiter and Venus. The wise men knew the scriptures, because Daniel became the head of all the wise men in Babylon, and so they understood the stars. All this information, I tucked away along with my childhood love of the stars, stars with which our magnificent Creator had adorned the night sky.

Skip forward about 15 years, and you'll find me travelling in my mini-van on the night of the 4th blood moon. I had stopped alongside the freeway to view the rusty colored eclipse of our nearest satellite when, through a strange set of circumstances, my van caught on fire!

I began looking for answers. I started watching the position of the moon and reading what the Bible had to say about the stars. As I watched each night the moon migrated, in its normal course over the next three weeks, to the opposite side of the sky. That's when the moon started to do something that filled my heart with wonder! It appeared to be moving towards a rendezvous with the Sun, several planets, the Virgin and a sign the Bible talks about in Revelation chapter 12! On October 14th, 2015, it reached the feet of the constellation Virgo, while Virgo (the virgin) was "clothed in the Sun".

But something was not quite right. I couldn't figure out certain parts of the prophecy. Where were the 12 stars that crowned her head? And which serpent or dragon constellation in the night sky represented the dragon who was waiting to devour the woman's child? Was this the fulfillment, or simply a dress-rehearsal? I began to search. I decided to look into the future, using a star-tracking program, just like the guy who found the Star of Bethlehem. What I found amazed me! I eventually landed in September of 2017, on an alignment of the planets, the Sun, Moon and stars, which fulfilled EVERY WORD of Revelation 12! EVERY WORD! I was excited and did an internet search of the dates. What I found was, there were other people who had discovered the same thing. I took that as a confirmation and began my research in earnest. The time was so short and while praying and seeking God, He kept showing me a scripture that said, "Open your mouth and I will fill it".

I found myself in the middle of the freeway, in the middle of the night, in the strange light of the blood moon, beating the flames out of my engine compartment with a length of fabric while side-by-side semi trucks roared past on either side of me, riding their air brakes! It was perhaps the strangest, most surreal and most dramatic event of my life. Needless to say, I had a few questions for God! Why did this happen? What are you trying to tell me? Am I supposed to pay attention to the stars?

So, here I am, writing the book of a lifetime, a book that has been waiting 5777 years to be written. I am opening my mouth, as I have been told. May those who have ears to hear, hear what I am about to say.

There are many more details that have come to light during the course of my research and I have done my best to detail them, cross-reference them and show the evidence that supports them, here for you. I will tell the story as simply as I can, including the more detailed and complicated information later in the book. There are still some unknowns, but I know one thing for certain, the Great and Wondrous Sign of Revelation Chapter 12 WILL happen in late September, 2017, letter for letter, word for word.

This is a message that I have been entrusted with. It is historic, epic. It is a message, not of the end, but of a new beginning, the birth pangs of The Kingdom of Jesus Christ coming to the Earth.

"Our Father, who art in Heaven, hallowed be thy name. Thy Kingdom come. Thy will be done, on Earth as it is in Heaven."

Revelation Chapter 12
The Woman and the Dragon

1 A great sign appeared in heaven: a woman clothed with the sun, with the moon under her feet and a crown of twelve stars on her head. 2 She was pregnant and cried out in pain as she was about to give birth. 3 Then another sign appeared in heaven: an enormous red dragon with seven heads and ten horns and seven crowns on its heads. 4 Its tail swept a third of the stars out of the sky and flung them to the earth. The dragon stood in front of the woman who was about to give birth, so that it might devour her child the moment he was born. 5 She gave birth to a son, a male child, who "will rule all the nations with an iron scepter."[a] And her child was snatched up to God and to his throne. 6 The woman fled into the wilderness to a place prepared for her by God, where she might be taken care of for 1,260 days.
7 Then war broke out in heaven. Michael and his angels fought against the dragon, and the dragon and his angels fought back.
8 But he was not strong enough, and they lost their place in heaven.
9 The great dragon was hurled down—that ancient serpent called the devil, or Satan, who leads the whole world astray. He was hurled to the earth, and his angels with him.
10 Then I heard a loud voice in heaven say:

"Now have come the salvation and the power
  and the kingdom of our God,
  and the authority of his Messiah.
For the accuser of our brothers and sisters,
  who accuses them before our God day and night,
  has been hurled down.
11 They triumphed over him
  by the blood of the Lamb
  and by the word of their testimony;
they did not love their lives so much
  as to shrink from death.
12 Therefore rejoice, you heavens
  and you who dwell in them!
But woe to the earth and the sea,
  because the devil has gone down to you!
He is filled with fury,
  because he knows that his time is short."

13 When the dragon saw that he had been hurled to the earth, he pursued the woman who had given birth to the male child.

14 The woman was given the two wings of a great eagle, so that she might fly to the place prepared for her in the wilderness, where she would be taken care of for a time, times and half a time, out of the serpent's reach. 15 Then from his mouth the serpent spewed water like a river, to overtake the woman and sweep her away with the torrent.

16 But the earth helped the woman by opening its mouth and swallowing the river that the dragon had spewed out of his mouth. 17 Then the dragon was enraged at the woman and went off to wage war against the rest of her offspring—those who keep God's commands and hold fast their testimony about Jesus.

Chapters

1. The Great and Wondrous Sign: Revelation 12:1-2
       a. The simple picture / story

2. How to watch the Great and Wondrous Sign in Sept.

3. The Lion
       a. Israel's Prophecy, "You are a lion's cub, oh Judah"

4. The Virgin

5. The Great Red Dragon
       I. Which constellation is the Dragon of Revelation
           a. Draco
           b. Others
           c. The Azure Dragon

6. The Leonids

7. Bible References to the Stars

Chapter 1

The Great and Wondrous Sign

Revelation 12:1-2
"A great and wondrous sign appeared in heaven: a woman clothed with the sun, with the moon under her feet and a crown of twelve stars on her head. She was pregnant and cried out in pain as she was about to give birth."

Let's look at this verse by verse and unpack what it says.

"A great and wondrous sign appeared in heaven: a woman clothed with the sun, with the moon under her feet and a crown of 12 stars on her head."

The language of the Bible always amazes me. It is so packed with information! First, it says, "A great and wondrous sign appeared in heaven". This sign is major; it is important and is intended to be marveled at, but also to cause us to consider, to wonder. What does it mean? The Scripture does not explain this sign directly and no angelic explanation is given as with some other visions, but we are invited to think about it, to probe deeply into its meaning.

Next, it says, "appeared in heaven". What does that mean? In the time and culture in which this was written, as well as from other clues in the context, this means "appeared in the night sky" or second Heaven. Here's how we know: in ancient times, biblical times, "the heavens" were divided (in their thinking) into three "heavens".

The first heaven was where the birds fly, between the Earth and the blue sky. This is what we refer to as the Earth's atmosphere. The second heaven is where the Sun, Moon and Stars reside, what we call "outer space". The third Heaven is where God's throne is, where angels and the spirits of those who are saved go when they die. The first two are visible to natural man and the third is spoken of often by prophets, such as when Paul says, in 2 Cor. 12:2-4, "I know a man in Christ who fourteen years ago was caught up to the third heaven. Whether it was in the body or out of the body I do not know—God knows. And I know that this man—whether in the body or apart from the body I do not know, but God knows— was caught up to paradise and heard inexpressible things, things that no one is permitted to tell."

The contextual clues establishing which "heaven" this sign appeared in, are when the passage talks about the Sun, Moon and stars. These objects are located in outer space, or again, what the ancients called "the second heaven". Also located in the second heaven, are the constellations that are spoken of, such as "a woman" who is able to be "clothed" in the Sun with the Moon "at her feet" and a crown of 12 stars "on her head". It directly implies that she is positioned in the sky in such a way that these objects cross her path. So, we need to ask, "Is there such a woman positioned in the night sky in a way that the sun and moon cross her path?" Yes, there is! When we put together all of these contextual clues, it is easy to identify the constellation Virgo, "the virgin" as a major part of the Great and Wondrous Sign. Virgo is located in the group of constellations through which the Sun, Moon and planets regularly travel.

The next part of this prophetic vision says, "She was pregnant and cried out in pain as she was about to give birth."

This too is symbolized in the night sky! Believe it or not, Jupiter, the King planet, which symbolizes the King of Kings, Jesus Christ, will be spending about 9 1/2 months in the belly of the constellation Virgo. To be clear, that's how long a pregnancy lasts. This is the kind of imagery that the Creator put into His creation. He designed men, women, childbirth and indeed the stars to tell a story which brings Him glory. Jupiter entered Virgo's belly at 5:14 AM on November 20th, 2016 and will be "born" September 9th at 1:54 AM. That's 293 days, or 9 months, 20 days. 42 weeks, a very full term pregnancy. Jesus spoke of these times when He compared the events of the last days to birth pangs. Mark 13:8b "These are the beginning of birth pains".

What I am excited to point out here, is representation of the birth of Jesus in the stars is only 14 days before the Great and Wondrous Sign. Also, I'd like to draw your attention to the fact that there is a complete eclipse of the Sun one month before the Great and Wondrous Sign on August 21st, 2017.

The prophet Joel is quoted by Peter,

Acts 2:17 "In the last days, God says, I will pour out my Spirit on all people. Your sons and daughters will prophecy, your young men will see visions, your old men will dream dreams. Even on my servants, both men and women I will pour out my Spirit in those days, and they will prophecy. I will show wonders in the heavens above and signs on the earth below, blood and fire and billows of smoke. The sun will be turned to darkness and the moon to blood before the coming of the great and glorious day of the Lord. And everyone who calls on the name of the Lord will be saved."

So, we know more about the stars already and how they relate to the Bible. Now, I'd like to show you a few diagrams of what I found! These are precise computer models of where the Sun, Moon and "stars" will be on September 22nd and 23rd, 2017. The planets move like clockwork and we are able to see where they will be at any point in the future. Here is a picture from the Stellarium software of what the Great and Wondrous Sign will look like.

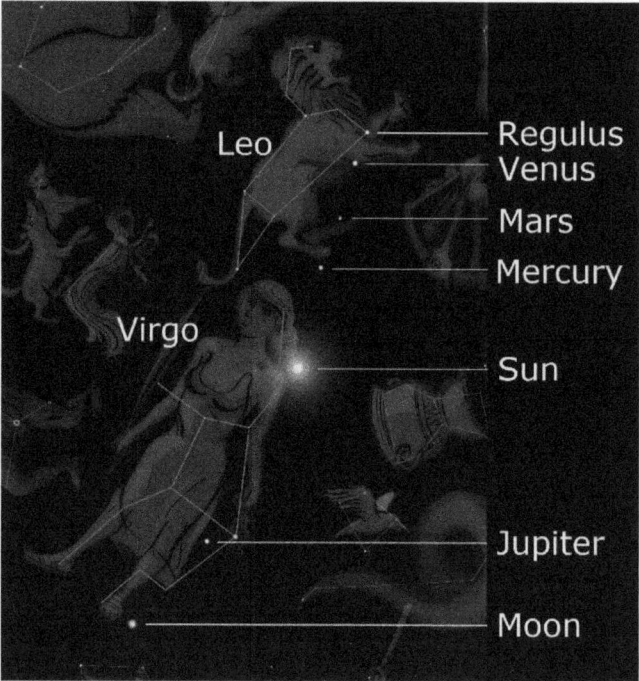

Stellarium images courtesy of Stellarium Developers, Copyright © 2000-2016

Below is a diagram of the Crown of 12 Stars (Tribes).

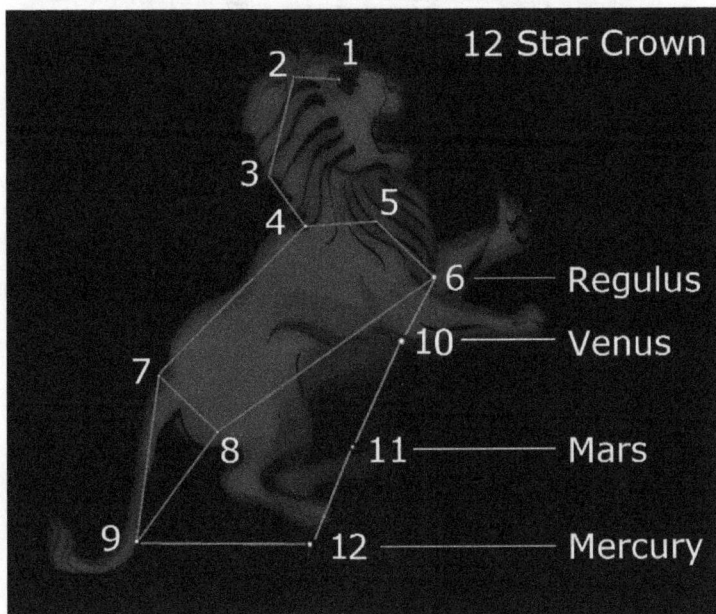

When lines are added to include the "wandering stars" or planets, it's easy to see the similarity to all the Egyptian crowns, but especiall to the "Pschent", which represented "ultimate authority". Many have speculated on where the crown was located, but as scripture says, the crown is "...a crown of 12 stars on her head." Also, notice the amazing alignment of the Sun, Moon, 4 planets and 2 stars! This is just historic!

Ring with the engraved portrait of Ptolemy VI Philometor, located in the Louvre, Paris France. This golden ring shows very clearly the combined crowns of upper and lower Egypt. It is very important to note that this crown was a sign of great power and ultimate authority for 3000 years.

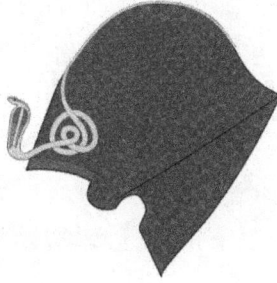

Khepresh

This is an example of an Egyptian Battle crown, showing   the   color.

"Elongated, rounded crown with a flared ridge passing around the back and studded with dotted circles. In reliefs and paintings its colour is shown as blue, a prestigious characteristic linked to the king in his active roles, in battle or carrying out rituals in the temples. The crown, which is known from the 18th Dynasty on, was also called the war crown, but this is probably inaccurate. The crown was probably made of leather or material with metal disks sewn onto it. The ancient Egyptian name for the crown was 'khepresh'." According to the Global Egyptian Museum.

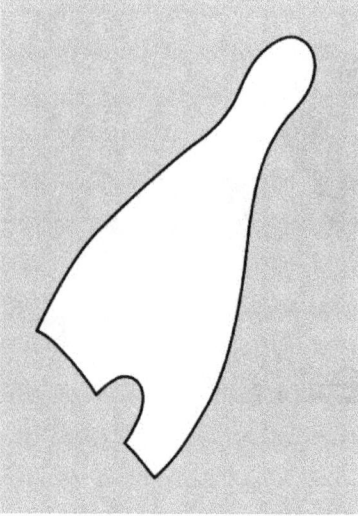

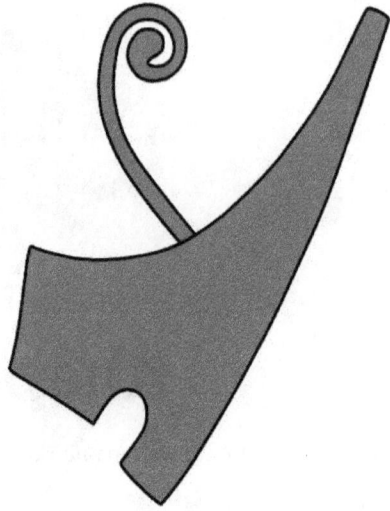

The crowns of Upper Egypt (Southern region, white) and Lower Egypt (Northern Region, red)

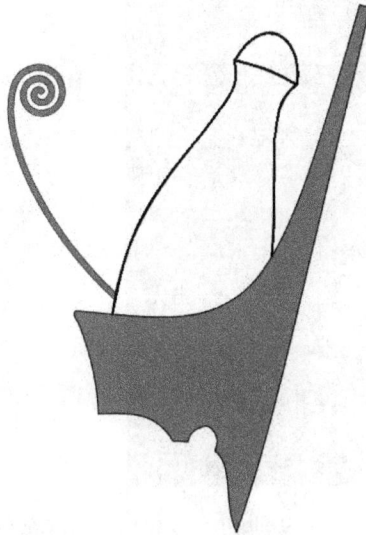

Here is the combined crowns of Upper and Lower Egypt, called the "Pschent", from when the Pharaoh ruled both regions. For 3000 years, this crown represented ultimate authority and kingship.

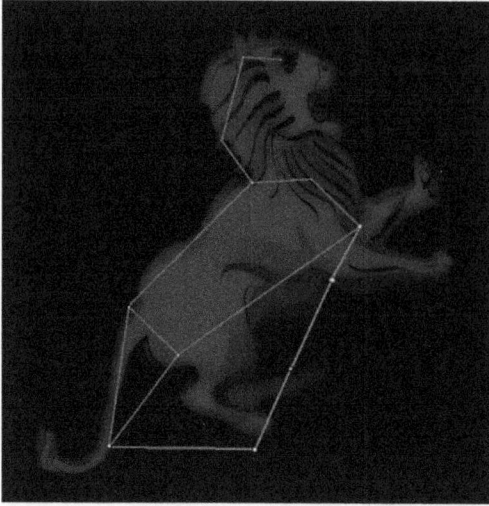

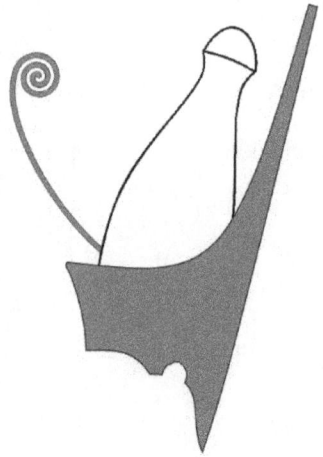

There is a lot of significance in the crown. The Lion of Judah is represented as Leo, with only 9 stars. It was a mystery to me where the other 3 stars would be, or what the crown really was. I prayed and asked God to show me what the truth was about the crown. Others have speculated about different nearby constellations, such as the Corona Borealis, however, it didn't quite work. When I was watching the planets come into alignment in 2015, there were 12 stars present, but not the right ones to convey the meaning of the prophecy in Revelation chapter 12. Since that time, I discovered the September 2017 alignment and it all makes perfect sense. Mercury and Jupiter have switched places in the alignment and Jupiter (the King) spends 9 1/2 months in Virgo's belly, instead of being part of the crown, in 2015, when what I call the "dress rehearsal" happened.

The 12 star crown represents the 12 Tribes of Israel. The three "wandering stars" (as planets were called) represent the three wandering tribes of Isreal that stayed on the East side of the Jordan. So this alignment represents a unified Israel (the crown), crowning the woman, who is a virgin (a symbol of purity) which I believe is the Church, the Bride of Christ. There are those that believe the woman is Israel. I lean away from this because of what the Bible says about Judah being represented by a lion, the location of the Star of Bethlehem and the interpretation the Magi gave to the constellation of Leo. Also, because if Israel is Leo (with 12 stars), then it isn't necessary to represent Israel by another constellation. It all makes sense, and the clues in scripture all come together when the woman is the Church, or Bride of Christ, a representation of all Christian believers. This is a huge key in understanding end times prophecy.

This implies many things. One of which is the woman fleeing into the wilderness would represent the rapture of the Church. Keep in mind that we will discuss how there are time tables which are variable. God has left it somewhat ambiguous and we will look at it in greater detail later.

Method of Interpreting the Stars

When looking at the story written in the stars, it's important to keep in mind that prophetic images are telling a story using powerful symbolism. Some parts of the story are physical, some may be metaphoric. Some parts are being retold and others are yet to come.

We will see how this particular set of signs is both talking about the original virgin birth of Jesus Christ, and His future return; the over-arching story of the hero (Messiah/Jesus) battling the antagonist (Dragon/Satan) both before time began, during the life of Christ and at the end of the age. In a sense, some of this moving diorama in the sky is thematic, yet, because it moves and the planets indicate "times" and "seasons", we can get a sense of plot motion in the story. It's good to reiterate, the Great and Wondrous Sign only happens once. The planets align this September and it hasn't happened exactly like this before - but it happens exactly as the Apostle John said in Revelation more than 2000 years ago!

Jupiter Represented the Messiah During the Life of Christ

The Hebrew name for Jupiter is "Sedeq". This word was also used, during the life of Jesus, as a term for the Messiah. So, if a Jewish scholar saw Jupiter in the belly of Virgo, it would indicate a virgin birth of the Messiah.

The Hebrew word "sedeq" means "rightness, righteousness;
1. what is right, just;
2. righteousness in government:
(a) of judges, rulers, kings
(b) of law
(c) of Davidic King, Messiah.
(d) of Jerusalem as seat of just government
(e) of God's attribute as sovereign
3. righteousness, justice in a case or cause; God judges according to righteousness
4. rightness in speech
5. righteousness, as ethically right 6. righteousness as vindicated, justification in

controversy with enemies and troubles, deliverance, victory, prosperity

(a) of God as covenant - keeping in redemption

(b) in name of Messianic King (vindicating people's cause and giving victory)

(c) of people as enjoying righteousness of salvation"

-Brown, Driver and Briggs, Hebrew-English Lexicon pages 841-842.

Applying this understanding of the stars to Scripture

Another detail that comes to mind is a passage where the Angel Gabriel announces the Immaculate Conception to Mary. So, I'm going to use this as an example because it is represented in the stars just prior to the Great and Wondrous Sign. I will try to explain how to interpret what the stars were saying in this event through the lens of scripture, to give you a sense of how I arrived at my interpretations.

Here is the scripture:
Luke 1:30-35

But the angel said to her, "Do not be afraid, Mary; you have found favor with God. You will conceive and give birth to a son, and you are to call him Jesus. He will be great and will be called the Son of the Most High. The Lord God will give him the throne of his father David, and he will reign over Jacob's descendants forever; his kingdom will never end."

"How will this be," Mary asked the angel, "since I am a virgin?"

The angel answered, "The Holy Spirit will come on you, and the power of the Most High will overshadow you. So, the holy one to be born will be called the Son of God."

It is important, here to point out that I am using the computer models to look ahead in time and see what the Sun, Moon and Stars are doing in the future (in this case Oct. - Nov., 2016 and beyond). Even more important is to note that I am using scripture to interpret these symbols, and NOT the other way around.

Here this part of the story in the Heavens:

Stellarium images courtesy of Stellarium Developers, Copyright © 2000-2016

As seen in a computer model above, just before Jupiter enters into Virgo, Virgo is visited by the Moon and is overshadowed by, or "clothed with" the Sun. Jupiter then enters Virgo's belly area and stays there for 9 1/2 months. This represents a "re-telling" of what happened during the Immaculate Conception, over 2000 years ago. Please note, this preceded the event of "The Great and Wondrous Sign" (which at the writing of this has not happened yet) by over 9 months.

Please keep in mind that we do not worship the Sun, Moon and Stars, but they can represent things symbolically, as we see in scripture. For example Judah is represented by Leo, the Lion. Sometimes in scripture, the sun represents "a bridegroom", other times; it can represent the power of God. Here are the symbolic meanings of each heavenly body for this passage, like characters in a play:

Jesus - represented by the King Planet, Jupiter (Hebrew: Sedeq or "Righteous One")

God - The Most High, represented by the greatest power in the sky, the Sun

Mary - represented by "the virgin", Virgo

Holy Spirit - represented by the Moon

So, here is the same prophecy (Luke 1:30-35) lined up exactly with the interpretation of the signs in the heavens:

Just before Jesus (Jupiter) enters into the Virgin Mary (Virgo) the Holy Spirit (the Moon) will come upon her and the power of the Most High (the Sun) will overshadow her. So symbolically, God (the Sun) visits Mary (Virgo) and His power overshadows her (causes the Immaculate Conception) and Jesus (Jupiter) spends 9 1/2 months in Mary's (Virgo's) belly.

Here is a visual representation of how this passage was interpreted:

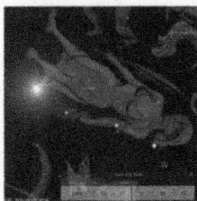

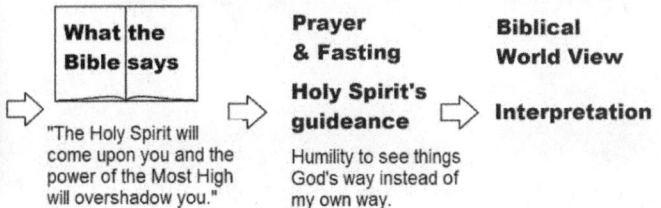

What the Bible says	Prayer & Fasting	Biblical World View
"The Holy Spirit will come upon you and the power of the Most High will overshadow you."	Holy Spirit's guideance Humility to see things God's way instead of my own way.	Interpretation

This is "seeing the stars through the lens of the scripture". This is the process I have used to interpret the rest of the signs. Not everyone is going to be able to "get it". Not everyone will believe what I have to share. This is a matter that perhaps only the Holy Spirit can reveal to each person in their own time. The main thing this sign is telling us is, "The time is short, even at the door."

Now, it's important to point out that this particular segment precedes the Great and Wondrous sign and is not directly labeled in the scripture as a sign to look for in the heavens. However, while studying the stars, you begin to see the story that is written there unfolding! Because I am familiar with Scripture, I started to see all the many similarities between the story in the stars and the familiar stories of the Bible.

When you look at it through the scripture, they are exactly the same! This kind of evidence that lines up with the narrative of scripture reinforces the Great and Wondrous sign and provides further evidence and support as well as grounding for our faith.

Just like the Wise Men saw the Star of Bethlehem and interpreted it by the scriptures where Jacob (Israel) blessed Judah, calling him a lion (Leo), and they arrived at a Biblical interpretation that was true (a King was born in Israel), I am attempting to do the same. (For more information on the Star of Bethlehem, please visit **www.bethlehemstar.com**)

Chapter 2.

How to watch
The Great and Wondrous Sign
in September

If you would like to view the Great and Wondrous Sign in the sky, much like the way the Magi saw the Star of Bethlehem, you will need to be out watching as the sun sets, and also before the sun rises. These were the times when the Magi recorded what was happening in the sky. This event cannot be fully observed without doing both the evening and the morning viewing.

The Great and Wondrous Sign will be visible in the western sky on the evening of September 22nd, 2017 and in the eastern sky early on the morning of September 23rd. This is the only time in history when it will happen. It will be on or near the horizon and only half of the sign is visible immediately after sunset and the other half, just before sunrise the next day. If you have a star tracking program on your smart phone or tablet, you will be able to see the sign on your device for the full duration of the event. A device can also help you to locate the upcoming event so you know where to look in the sky, as well as when to be at your viewing area. I recommend an area away from city lights, where you can see the horizon unobstructed by mountains or clouds, if possible.

If you track the Sun, Moon and planets for a few days before the event, you will be able to watch them coming into alignment, a process that promises to be very exciting and rewarding!

Practicing will also ensure you know where to look and what you are looking for. It takes some familiarity to be able to find the constellations and planets in the night   sky.

The following diagrams are EXACTLY what you are looking for. These depict "The Great and Wondrous Sign":

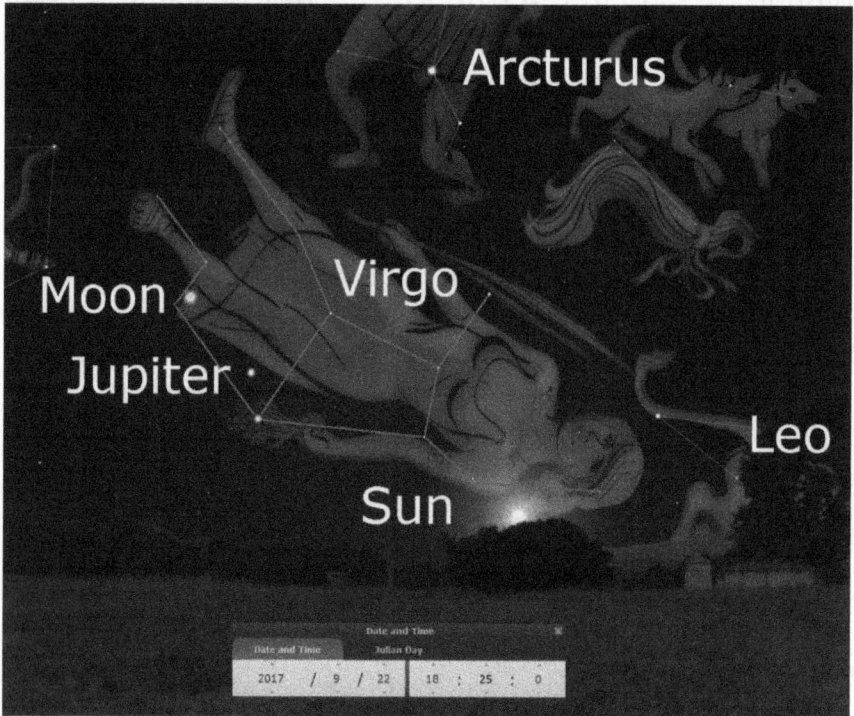

This illustration shows the first part of the sign, viewed in the evening of September 22nd, as the sun is setting.

Of course, the helpful illustration of Virgo will not be in the sky, so I have included below two more versions of the same moment in time, to help you be familiar with both the constellations and the appearance of them in the sky without any artificial lines or artistic interpretations.

Stellarium images courtesy of Stellarium Developers, Copyright © 2000-2016

This illustration shows the constellation Virgo with the Moon at her feet, Jupiter having exited her belly area and the sun about to set in the West. It is helpful to be familiar with the shape of the lines, which helps to identify the constellation when you look at the stars.

Stellarium images courtesy of Stellarium Developers, Copyright © 2000-2016

So! Here's the challenge! Can you identify the shape of Virgo from the previous illustrations? This is approximately what the sky will look like as the sun goes down and the stars come out. The stars will be a little harder to see than this illustration, because the sun may cause interference until after it has gone down. But you should be able to see the moon, and below it, Jupiter having been "born" from the Virgin. This is the first part of the Great and Wondrous Sign. Perhaps the next morning's event will look more impressive to the bare eye, with the alignment of Regulus, Venus, Mars and Mercury, making up the crown.

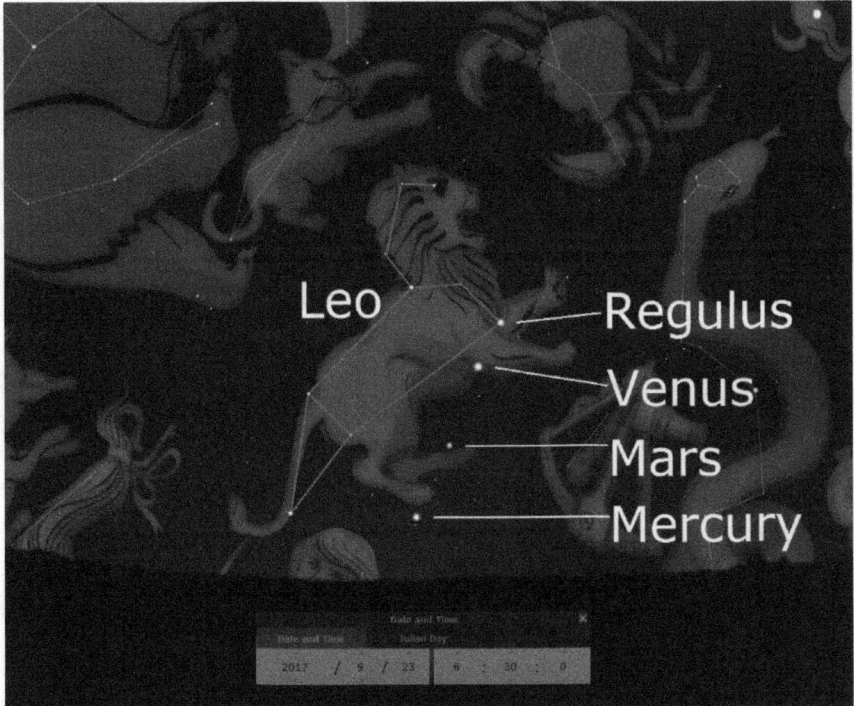

This is what to look for in the sky on the morning of September 23rd BEFORE the Sun rises. Leo begins to rise at 3:20 AM and the whole thing is finished by 6:20 AM. It may seem very early, but it only happens once! Knowing the significance of this event should add abundant motivation to see it actually taking place. Those who view the event can treasure it, as when the angel announced the birth of Christ and Mary treasured these things in her heart. You'll be able to say, "I was THERE! I saw that with my own eyes!" This is the fulfillment of a prophecy that is highly significant and has been waiting 2000+ years to be fulfilled.

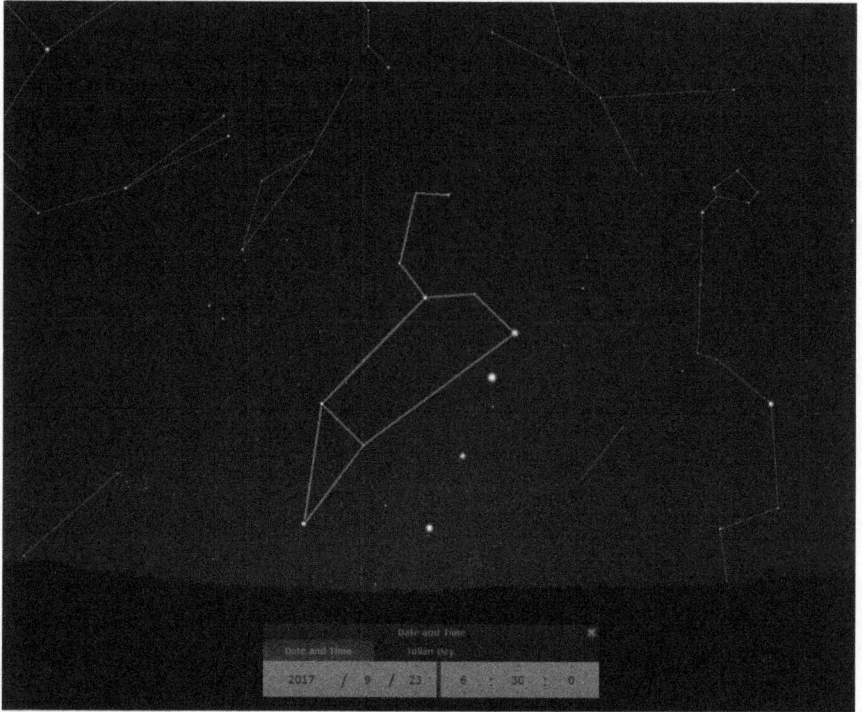

Study the shapes of the constellations in these illustrations. They will help you identify the correct place in the sky, so you won't miss the event. Leo will rise in the East several hours before sunrise.

Stellarium images courtesy of Stellarium Developers, Copyright © 2000-2016

This is perhaps the most significant alignment to happen during our lifetime. What you're looking for is Leo and the 3 planets that align with Regulus. The Magi would have been beside themselves with excitement to witness this! Trace the shape of Leo in your mind. I find the head of Leo an easy shape to identify, with its 5 stars shaped like a sickle. Below that, Regulus is the brightest star in the constellation and will precede the three planets of Venus (very bright), Mars (slightly red) and Mercury (least bright and perhaps hard to see as the Sun will soon rise). Please do not stare at the sun when it starts rising, unless you saved your eclipse glasses, which should checked for any damage.

Chapter 3

The Lion

Gen. 49:8-12

"Judah, your brothers will praise you;
    your hand will be on the neck of your enemies;
    your father's sons will bow down to you.
You are a lion's cub, Judah;
    you return from the prey, my son.
Like a lion he crouches and lies down,
    like a lioness—who dares to rouse him?
The scepter will not depart from Judah,
    nor the ruler's staff from between his feet,
until he to whom it belongs shall come
    and the obedience of the nations shall be his.
He will tether his donkey to a vine,
    his colt to the choicest branch;
he will wash his garments in wine,
    his robes in the blood of grapes.
His eyes will be darker than wine,
    his teeth whiter than milk.

This prophetic blessing, which Israel bestowed upon his son, foretells the coming of a ruler called "Shiloh" also interpreted as "he to whom it belongs", a title given to the Messiah. This ruler would be a descendant of the tribe of Judah. As Christians, we can clearly see that this was a vision of the Messiah, Jesus   Christ.

What I want to draw out from this, is a discovery I made while researching the Star of Bethlehem. According to Bethlehemstar.org, and confirmed by my own research into the subject, the Star of Bethlehem was formed by a significant conjunction of Jupiter and Saturn, so close that it formed what looked like one super bright star, which moved back and forth over Regulus, the "regal" or "king star" in the constellation Leo. By comparing this motion to the scripture above, moving back and forth, the Star of Bethlehem formed a line that could be interpreted as a scepter or "ruler's staff" near the star known as Regulus (the "regal" or kingly star) in the front legs Leo.

This must have been how the Magi knew a king was born in Israel. How did they figure out what the stars were saying? It is widely accepted that Daniel, while in Babylon, had with him copies of the books of the Law of Moses, Genesis - Deuteronomy. The Magi or wise men were highly educated men and advisers to their king on world affairs. They studied important documents, kept detailed records of the stars, eclipses of the sun and moon and other such signs in the heavens, from which they were actually able to predict future events! (as evidenced by their journey to find Jesus)

Since Daniel was the top adviser to four consecutive kings, the wise men under his authority would obviously be familiar with the Hebrew scriptures and would have trained their successors accordingly. When they witnessed the Star of Bethlehem, it would have been the brightest star they had seen in their lifetime, so naturally, they were intent on finding out what it could mean. When the star moved back and forth over Regulus, forming what could be interpreted as a staff or scepter, they would only have to ask themselves, "Where have we heard of a lion with a staff or a scepter?" They would have realized that Genesis said something about Judah being a lion and having a scepter between his feet!

Thus, a scepter formed by the King planet near the King star, in the King constellation was telling the Magi, "Shiloh - the Messiah - the King of Kings is born in Israel!" Not only that, but it would later depart when "Shiloh" comes. This whole event in the stars is what prompted them to travel to the Land of Israel, and ask, "Where is the one who has been born King of the Jews? We saw his star in the East and have come to worship him." Two years later, the star reappeared (re-conjuncted) and the Magi were overjoyed. The second conjunction stopped over the house where Jesus was and the Magi presented him with gifts of gold, frankincense and myrrh. (Matt. 2:1-12)

So, here we are, two thousand and some years later and things which are foretold in the scripture are beginning to happen in the night sky! **THIS IS EXCITING STUFF!!**

Three Wise men: used under license © 2017 James E. McConnell / Look and Learn Ltd.

It is important to note that the Magi could tell many different facts from the stars. They knew a King was born. They could tell what country He would be in. They could tell events were happening on the Earth at the same time as they were happening in the stars. They could even find the house where the child was living.

Let's ponder that! This is not a fairy tale. This actually happened!

Chapter 4

The Virgin

Revelation 12:1-2

"A great sign appeared in heaven: a woman clothed with the sun, with the moon under her feet and a crown of twelve stars on her head. She was pregnant and cried out in pain as she was about to give birth."

(NOTE: I came back to this chapter to add this: This is my original research and only after I came to these discoveries was I able to find other people online who also came to the same conclusions about Virgo and the crown of 12 stars. In fact, I had written this chapter before I found anyone with the same idea. I am grateful that God has revealed these things not only to me, because the word needed to get out to the church! I believe this to be confirmation that I am on the right track and my method of interpreting the stars is both valid and effective. I say this not to boast, but to give insight into what I believe is knowledge that has been revealed to us in the last days. Praise God.)

Bethulah, the Hebrew word for "virgin", is what the people of Israel called the constellation Virgo. It is one of the 12 constellations of the Hebrew Mazaroth.

"But you, Bethlehem Ephratha, though you are small among the clans of Judah, out of you will come for me one who will be ruler over Israel, whose origins are from of old, from ancient times (from days of eternity) Therefore Israel will be abandoned until the time when she who is in labor gives birth and the rest of his brothers return to join the Israelites." Micah 5:2-3

This passage talks about several key times in history all at once, as many prophecies do. This is often referred to as the "Hilltops of Prophecy", in which a prophet sees a vision of the future, but it is actually multiple events reverberating through time. First and foremost, it refers to the virgin birth, the birth of the Messiah, as it says "whose origins are from of old, from ancient times". It speaks of one who is eternal being born of a virgin! A real mystery to them at the time! But we know who it is referring to: Jesus Christ, the incarnation of God. All this is correct and good, but this prophecy also projects further into the future. It is also speaking of the stars and what would be acted out in the Great and Wondrous Sign as well as using these images as a metaphor for Israel, the Church, and end times events on the Earth. Where it says, "until the time when she who is in labor gives birth and the rest of his brothers return to join the Israelites." it is also referring to several things:

1. Revelation 12:1-2, "...and a crown of 12 stars on her head." (explained below)
2. The return of the Jews to the Holy Land, "...and the rest of his brothers return to join the Israelites."
3. When "she who is in labor", refers to the suffering of the end times, the persecution of God's people.

The crown of 12 stars correlates to the 12 tribes of Israel. The verse from Micah which says, "and the rest of his brothers return to join the Israelites" helps us to interpret and identify the stars of which Revelation 12 speaks. There is a bit of a mystery here too, because the 9 stars of Leo (the Lion of Judah above the head of Virgo) obviously do not fulfill the prophecy of "a crown of 12 stars" and have left many scholars guessing at which stars the prophecy is referring to. I prayed and asked God for wisdom, insight and understanding and He revealed the meaning of this mystery. It is only when the 9 stars of Leo, which represents the 9 tribes that settled on the West side of the Jordan, are joined by the 3 wandering stars (planets) to make 12 stars in the crown, that we can clearly interpret the prophecy, with a crown of 12 stars representing the 12 tribes of Israel. The three wandering stars represent the three "wandering" tribes of Israel that stayed on the East side of the Jordan. They are Mercury, Venus and Mars, which line up in the Great and Wondrous Sign to make a complete 12 star crown, when combined with the 9 stars of Leo. As a side note, there could be a point at which these tribes ("the rest of his brothers" scattered among the nations) join with Israel in the near future, most likely in the rebuilding of The Temple. Many of the articles required for temple worship have been researched and reconstructed. At present, there are disputes about where the temple was. I've seen evidence that suggests that the large platform usually referred to as "the temple mount" is actually the remains of a Roman fortress built near the temple mount. Be watching for an archaeological discovery that places the temple mount nearby, because at that point, the Jews will rebuild the temple and prophetic events will unfold quite rapidly.

Matthew 24:30 The sign of the Son of Man

"How shall these things be, since I am a virgin?"

The Holy Spirit will come upon you and the power of the Most High will overshadow you, and so the holy one to be born will be called, "The Son of God".

This is interesting, because in Revelation 12, it says the virgin will be clothed in the Sun. In terms of the Sun, Moon and stars, the Sun is "the most high" and when Virgo is clothed in the sun, she is "overshadowed" and cannot be seen, because of the power of the 'most high'. If the Holy Spirit is represented by the Moon, then this prophetic verse also plays out in the stars, because the moon comes into contact with Virgo, then eclipses Jupiter 1 hour later, then Jupiter enters Virgo's belly for 9 1/2 months, analogous to a human pregnancy. Here's the timeline of the stars:

9-13-2016 The Sun begins to overshadow Virgo (present through 11-5-16), so she cannot be seen.

9-30-2016 at 9:24 AM, the Moon "comes upon" Virgo (but would not overshadow, so a different term is used)

9-30-2016 at 10:24 AM, the Moon eclipses Jupiter (Just one hour after it starts to, and continues to touch Virgo)

11-20-2016 at 5:15 AM, Jupiter (the King) enters Virgo (the virgin) for 9 1/2 months!

Isaiah 7:14 "Therefore the Lord himself will give you a sign: behold, a virgin shall conceive, and bear a son, and shall call his name Immanuel.

There are so many implications and metaphors going on, as these heavenly bodies interact. The Moon eclipsing Jupiter could be interpreted "the Holy Spirit" (Life of God) touches Jupiter and Virgo at the same time, as if bonding them together, and imparting this immaculate conception with life!

Matthew 1:18

"This is how the birth of Jesus the Messiah came about: His mother Mary was pledged to be married to Joseph, but before they came together, she was found to be pregnant through the Holy Spirit. Because Joseph her husband was faithful to the law, and yet did not want to expose her to public disgrace, he had in mind to divorce her quietly. But after he had considered this, an angel of the Lord appeared to him in a dream and said, "Joseph son of David, do not be afraid to take Mary home as your wife, because what is conceived in her is from the Holy Spirit. She will give birth to a son, and you are to give him the name Jesus, because he will save his people from their sins." All this took place to fulfill what the Lord had said through the prophet: "The virgin will conceive and give birth to a son, and they will call him Immanuel (which means "God with us"). When Joseph woke up, he did what the angel of the Lord had commanded him and took Mary home as his wife. But he did not consummate the marriage until she gave birth to a son. And he gave him the name Jesus."

Isaiah 9:6 "For unto us a child is born, unto us a son is given; and the government shall be upon his shoulder: and his name shall be called Wonderful, Counselor, Mighty God, Everlasting Father, Prince of Peace. Of the increase of his government and of peace there shall be no end, upon the throne of David, and upon his kingdom to establish it, and to uphold it with justice and with righteousness from henceforth even forever. The zeal of the Lord of Hosts will perform this."

Isaiah informs us that the child to be born is not just "the Son of God", but that he shall be called "Mighty God, Everlasting Father". The child to be born is fully God, come to live among us, "Emanuel" - God with us!

1 Thessalonians 5:3

"For when they shall say, Peace and safety; then sudden destruction cometh upon them, as travail (labor pains) upon a woman with child; and they shall not escape."

This is a very important passage in Thessalonians; The Apostle Paul refers metaphorically to the Great and Wondrous Sign. Scripture does this sort of thing very often. It's imperative to interpret scripture by other scripture, or else we get a skewed perspective on what certain passages mean. Could this passage imply that "The Day of the Lord" will come near the time of the Great and Wondrous Sign? If we compare it to Revelation 12:1-2, "A great sign appeared in heaven: a woman clothed with the sun, with the moon under her feet and a crown of twelve stars on her head. 2 She was pregnant and cried out in pain as she was about to give birth." we notice a number of obvious similarities:

1. They both deal with the End Times
2. They both talk about a woman "with child" or "pregnant" (same thing)
3. They both mention labor pains

There are vital questions that need to be addressed because of 1 Thes. 5:3, as it relates to Rev. 12:1-2, because 1 Thes. implies that the labor pains in Revelation 12 may be referring to "destruction cometh upon them". We have to consider, who does the Virgin represent? What are those labor pains? Franklin Graham recently shared an article showing that 215 million Christians experienced "extreme persecution" in 2016 and as many as 90,000 worldwide were martyred for their faith.
https://billygraham.org/story/franklin-graham-persecution-on-an-unprecedented-scale/
It's not hard to see that we are living in the end times. If the Church is the Virgin, and her crown is Israel, we can clearly see how this fits our current situation. Both the Church and Israel are being actively persecuted.
This brings me to another point: why do I believe the Virgin is the Church?
1. Israel is already, historically represented by the constellation Leo. (See chapter 3 "The Lion")
2. When the Virgin flees into the dessert, it is analogous to the Children of Israel fleeing from Pharaoh, into the wilderness of Sinai. However, the analogy doesn't end there. Israel also is a metaphor for the Church.
So if Leo is the nation of Israel, then the Virgin fleeing into the dessert would represent the Church "being caught up" into the 3rd Heaven for the 3 1/2 to 7 years (depending on your viewpoint) during the Tribulation period, commonly referred to as "The Rapture".

It's no coincidence that the Virgin flees into the dessert for a time, times and half a time (3 1/2 years), or that 40 years is also very closely resembled by 42 months in a 3 1/2 year period.

This passage is so important, I want to include it in its entirety:

1 Thessalonians 5 (NIV)

The Day of the Lord

1 Now, brothers and sisters, about times and dates we do not need to write to you, 2 for you know very well that the day of the Lord will come like a thief in the night. 3 While people are saying, "Peace and safety," destruction will come on them suddenly, as labor pains on a pregnant woman, and they will not escape.

4 But you, brothers and sisters, are not in darkness so that this day should surprise you like a thief. 5 You are all children of the light and children of the day. We do not belong to the night or to the darkness. 6 So then, let us not be like others, who are asleep, but let us be awake and sober. 7 For those who sleep, sleep at night, and those who get drunk, get drunk at night. 8 But since we belong to the day, let us be sober, putting on faith and love as a breastplate, and the hope of salvation as a helmet. 9 For God did not appoint us to suffer wrath but to receive salvation through our Lord Jesus Christ. 10 He died for us so that, whether we are awake or asleep, we may live together with him. 11 Therefore encourage one another and build each other up, just as in fact you are doing.

I truly hope that is what this book does. I hope it builds up the church and encourages all of us. Keep watching and waiting for the return of Jesus! Keep in mind that the labor pains are something that is telling us, "Here He comes!"

Just like when a woman is in labor. Let it remind us to walk in the light, as He is in the light - to purify ourselves and rid our lives of sin. This passage reminds us that "God did not appoint us to suffer [His] wrath" which is poured out in the second half of the Tribulation, lasting 3 1/2 years, referred to as "The Great and Terrible Tribulation". During the first 3 1/2 of the Tribulation period, there is a peace treaty. Then, half way through the 7 year period, the Anti-Christ enters the Holy of Holies and declares himself to be "god".

Chapter 5

The Great Red Dragon
(The Second Sign)

Revelation 12:3-4

"Then another sign appeared in heaven: an enormous red dragon with seven heads and ten horns and seven crowns on its heads. 4 Its tail swept a third of the stars out of the sky and flung them to the earth. The dragon stood in front of the woman who was about to give birth, so that it might devour her child the moment he was   born...

Revelation 12:7-9 Then war broke out in heaven. Michael and his angels fought against the dragon, and the dragon and his angels fought back. 8 But he was not strong enough, and they lost their place in heaven. 9 The great dragon was hurled down—that ancient serpent called the devil, or Satan, who leads the whole world astray. He was hurled to the earth, and his angels   with   him...

Revelation 12:12-17
Therefore rejoice, you heavens
    and you who dwell in them!
But woe to the earth and the sea,
    because the devil has gone down to you!
He is filled with fury,

because he knows that his time is short."When the dragon saw that he had been hurled to the earth, he pursued the woman who had given birth to the male child. 14 The woman was given the two wings of a great eagle, so that she might fly to the place prepared for her in the wilderness, where she would be taken care of for a time, times and half a time, out of the serpent's reach. 15 Then from his mouth the serpent spewed water like a river, to overtake the woman and sweep her away with the torrent. 16 But the earth helped the woman by opening its mouth and swallowing the river that the dragon had spewed out of his mouth. 17 Then the dragon was enraged at the woman and went off to wage war against the rest of her offspring—those who keep God's commands and hold fast their testimony about Jesus.

Which constellation is the Dragon of Revelation 12?
Is it Draco?

"Then another sign appeared in heaven: an enormous red dragon with seven heads and ten horns and seven crowns on his heads. His tail swept a third of the stars out of the sky and flung them to the earth. The dragon stood in front of the woman who was about to give birth, so that he might devour her child the moment it was born. She gave birth to a son, a male child, who will rule all the nations with an iron scepter. And her child was snatched up to God and to his throne. The woman fled into the desert to a place prepared for her by God, where she might be taken care of for 1260 days."

It occurs to me, the identity of the Great Red Dragon, much like the identity of the Anti-Christ, was hidden until the end times. I suspect the identity of the Anti-Christ should soon be revealed, perhaps in conjunction with the passing of this sign.

Solving the mystery of the great red dragon was difficult and complex. No one else seemed to have found this answer, so I inquired of the Lord. After much research and searching, I have concluded that there are two constellations that represent the dragon being spoken of in Revelation 12. The first is the constellation Draco (pronounced DRAY-co) coming from the Latin word which means "Dragon". This constellation rotates around the north star, proceeding tail first (counter clockwise), and takes 1 year to "sweep" approximately 1/3 of the night sky with it's tail. As I was discovering this information, which seemed an obvious fulfillment of portions of Revelation 12, having multiple heads and sweeping 1/3 of the "starry host" (representing angels), it clearly did not fit, in relation to being at the feet of the Virgin. Here, I want to mention that I also was realizing that the Leonids (a meteor shower originating from the area of Leo) happened in concert with the alignments, the tail sweeping, etc. I wondered over this and I believe it represents the 1/3 of the angels that God (represented by Leo) cast to the Earth with Satan. So, Draco fulfills PART of the prophecy in Revelation 12 but not all of it. Here are the verses I believe Draco fits with:

Revelation 12:7 Then war broke out in heaven. Michael and his angels fought against the dragon, and the dragon and his angels fought back. 8 But he was not strong enough, and they lost their place in heaven. 9 The great dragon was hurled down—that ancient serpent called the devil, or Satan, who leads the whole world astray. He was hurled to the earth, and his angels with him.

Draco, according to tradition, is a serpent coils around the star that never moves, the Pole Star, or North Star, which is rumored to be "The Gateway to Heaven" and immortality, representing the Tree of Life. Even Cephas (St. Peter) is a constellation that is seated nearby, implying that Peter too, is guarding the Pearly Gates.

Draco

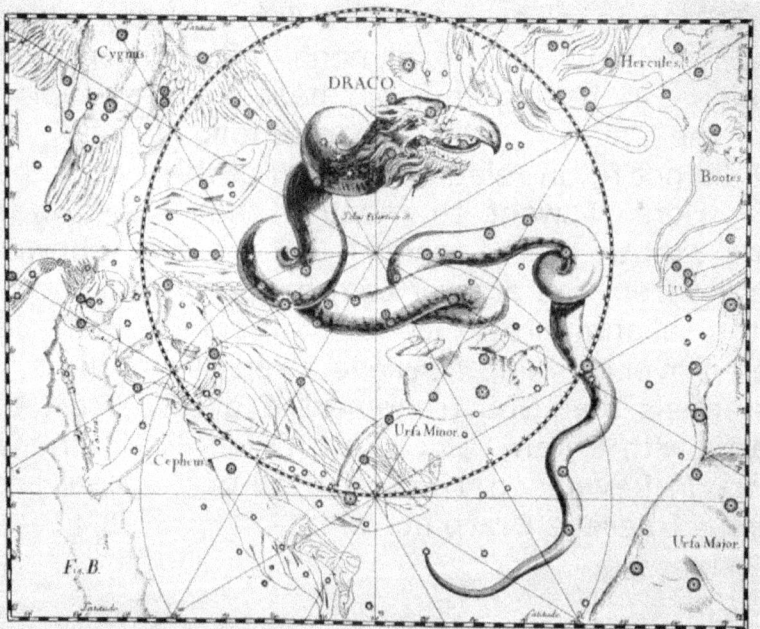

Fair Use, The constellation Draco from Firmamentum Sobiescianum sive Uranographia by Johannes Hevelius, 1690

In Greek mythology the dragon is Landon, the guardian of the "golden apples" of immortality that grew in the garden of Hesperiedes, beyond the river Time, in the land of death. Sound familiar? Like the tree of life, in the garden of Eden? (Hercules kills the dragon to get the golden apples and thus, immortality).

Another scripture that is fulfilled in the sky, concerning Draco, is this: "and I will put enmity between your offspring and hers; he will crush your head, and you will strike his heel." (or bruise his heel)

This is visible in the sky as Draco's head is directly under Hercules's heel. In some sense, God's original meaning of Hercules would be the conquering Messiah, Jesus, who as the seed of the woman is crushing Satan, the Serpent's head under His foot. One interesting detail is, it says God will put enmity between the woman's Seed (capital letter denoting a proper name - the Messiah) and *the Serpent's seed* which would suggest that not only the Christ was prophesied in Genesis chapter 3, but also the seed of Satan, possibly the Anti-Christ. (This just occurred to me.)   Here   is   the   scripture:

Genesis 3:14-15 (NKJV)

The first prophecy about the Messiah
So the Lord God said to the serpent:
"Because you have done this, you are cursed more than all cattle,
And more than every beast of the field;
On your belly you shall go,
And you shall eat dust all the days of your life.
And I will put enmity between you and the woman,

And between your seed and her Seed; He shall bruise your head,
And you shall bruise His heel."

This passage is quite prominently represented in the stars and constellations. In the following illustration, Hercules is clearly seen with his heal prominently over the head of Draco, poised to crush it. In fact, the legend of Hercules as well as the picture we see below represents him battling with a serpent, so the original meaning has not been completely lost.

So, that's the main significance of Draco. It is not located at the feet of the Virgin, so it is obviously not "The Great Red Dragon" of Revelation 12:1-3

Because Draco didn't fulfill ALL of the prophecy, I continued to search the constellations for a dragon or a serpent that would fit the proximity requirement to be waiting at the feet of the virgin, but in the sky there were only Libra and below that Scorpio. At first, when I looked at them, I suspected that the scorpion's very recognizable tail might be part of a dragon, and over the millennia, may have been called different things, as research suggested. So, I researched these two constellations and traced their origin back from the Greeks and Egyptians, to the Babylonians and then to the Chinese star charts. The Chinese have completely different constellations than the Greeks and also different from most of the Western World.

But they had one constellation that caught my attention right away! Their chief constellation, and indeed their national symbol appearing on many ancient Chinese flags was a dragon! Not just any dragon. A dragon made up of what we know as Scorpio and Libra, resting precisely at the feet of Virgo! Not only that, but as the Sun, Moon and planets move through the constellations, they go through Leo, then Virgo and into this Chinese dragon, known as the "Azure Dragon". That meant that after Jupiter (the King planet - representing Jesus Christ) spends 9 1/2 months in Virgo's belly He enters the mouth of the Azure Dragon, who is "waiting to devour the child"! But, not only that, as He enters the mouth of the dragon, something spectacular happens! Mars, the planet of war, conjuncts with Jupiter symbolizing The King of Kings bringing war against the Dragon!

Libra is a symbol of the set of scales based on the Scales of Justice held by Themis, the Greek personification of divine law and custom. In other words, Jesus has weighed Satan's guilt on the Scales of Justice. It's interesting to note that the scales are actually part of the Dragon. Satan is called the "accuser of the brethren" and God's judgment against Satan is inherent to who Satan is. I was so excited! This was such a revelation! I can't tell you how excited I was to find all this in the stars! Every bit fits! Every word of prophecy will be played out to the letter. God is showing us a picture book story, in the sky, of His plan.

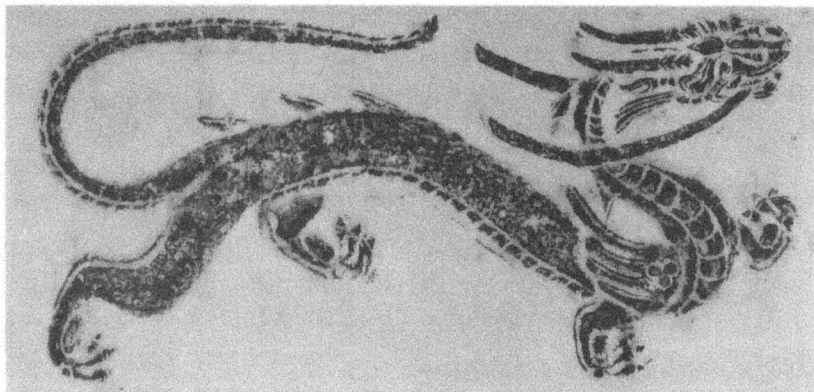

© The Field Museaum of Natural History, A96234, David Crockett Graham D.Sc., Ph.D., B.D., F.R.G.S., who was an American Missionary to China.

Description: Chinese rubbing of Azure Dragon from tomb of Wang Hui. Stone coffin, east side. Hsi-k'ang (extension of Szechwan during Han), Lu-shan. Rubbing collected by D.C.Graham in the 1940s and contributed to The Field Museum around 1957. Source: Extracted from pdf file of "Catalogue of Chinese Rubbings from Field Museum." Date: 1981, Author: Field Museum of Natural History. "David Crockett Graham (葛維漢, Ge Weihan, his Chinese name), D.Sc., Ph.D., B.D., F.R.G.S. (21 March 1884 – 15 September 1961) was a polymath American Baptist minister and missionary, educator, author, archeologist, anthropologist, naturalist and field collector in Szechuan Province, West China from 1911 to 1948." - http://www.wikiwand.com/en/David_Crockett_Graham

Figure 1

Composite image by David M. Willhite, © The Field Museaum of Natural History, A96234, © 2017 , Stellarium images courtesy of Stellarium Developers, Copyright © 2000-2016

Here I have overlaid the rubbing from the ancient Chinese tomb to show how well it lines up with the constellations. Virgo is in yellow, the official elements of the Azure Dragon are in RED. The light blue is what I think could have been part of the constellation, as it resembles the rubbing. Notice how the curve of the neck matches the "neck stars" as the Chinese refer to them, and the tail somewhat matches the stars as well, plus the characteristic curve of the back. The red rhombus shape to the top left of the tail is called "The basket" and for reasons unknown to me, the line connecting Virgo's "hips" is considered to be the "horns" of the dragon.

The arching back and curving neck and tail are all features of the Azure Dragon that are consistent in various artistic representations, and here I have demonstrated that the similarity is because it matches the shape of the stars in the constellation.

There really is no controversy about the Azure Dragon's location; it is most definitely located at the feet of Virgo, as the scriptures predicted. Names of constellations have changed from culture to culture, but the meaning of most of them has actually been somewhat preserved. The Great Red Dragon presented a mystery, but I think it is now solved.

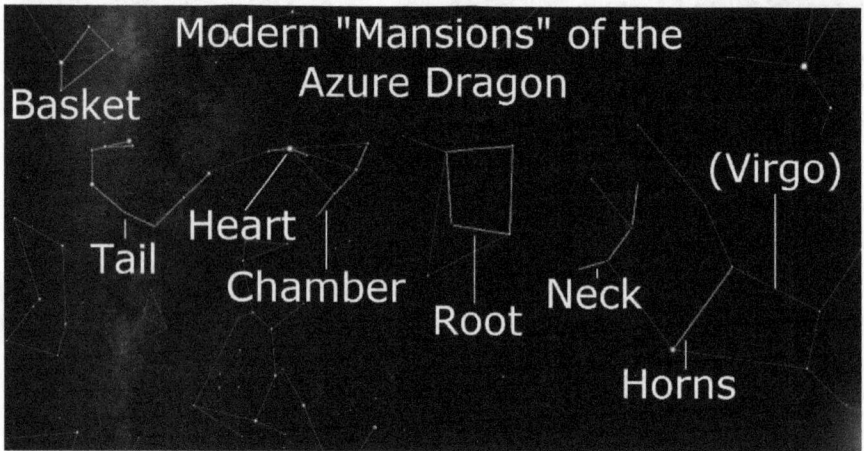

Figure 2 Based on information from
http://idp.bl.uk/education/astronomy/sky.html

Above, we can see the modern Chinese asterisms that make up the Azure Dragon (The Great Red Dragon, for our purposes). Each asterism, or group of stars, represents a "mansion" or station of the Moon as it passes through the constellation.

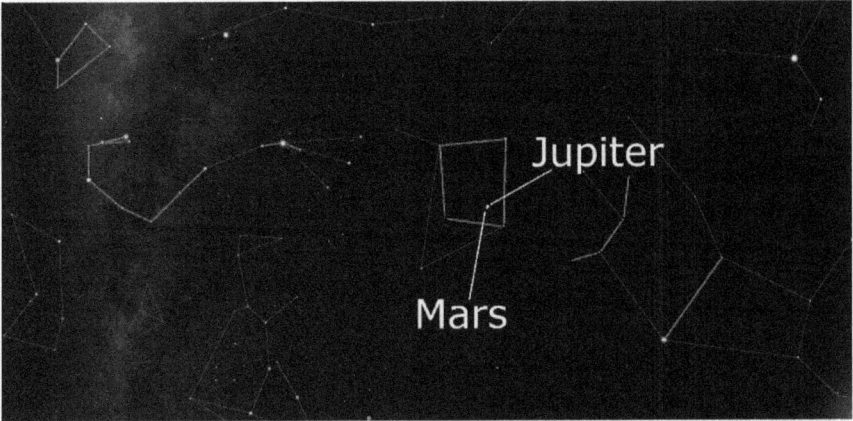

Figure 3 Stellarium images courtesy of Stellarium Developers, Copyright © 2000-2016

Here we have Jupiter and Mars in very, very close conjunction. This is the part where Christ brings war against the Dragon. I discovered this conjunction using the Stellarium software. The conjunction of Jupiter and Mars will take place on January 6th, 2018. Keep in mind that I am not "date setting". Just because the events take place in the stars, does not mean that events take place simultaneously on the Earth. But I do believe they take place soon after.

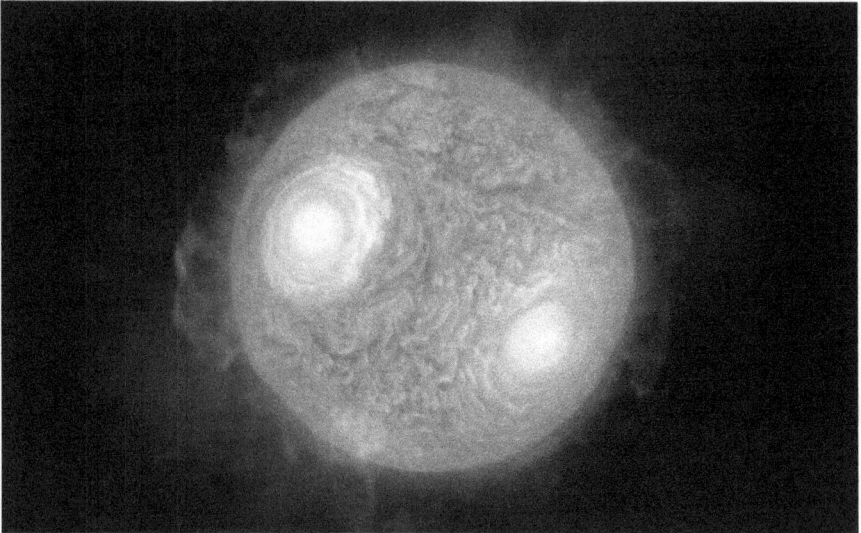

"This artist's impression shows the red supergiant star Antares in the constellation of Scorpius. Using ESO's Very Large Telescope Interferometer astronomers have constructed the most detailed image ever of this, or any star other than the Sun. Using the same data they have also made the first map of the velocities of material the atmosphere of a star other than the Sun." - ESO

The "Heart of the Dragon" is made up of three stars, the brightest of which is Antares, a red super-giant (depicted above) that has a distinct red glow. I believe this is why the Bible refers to the Dragon as "The Great Red Dragon". It is about 550 light-years away and is about 12 times larger than the Sun. Antares is the 15th brightest star in the night sky and scientists have recently discovered that it is in the last stages before it goes Super Nova.

This is significant in my thinking, because it represents Christ's final victory over Satan (and just to be clear, The Great Red Dragon represents Satan).

Antares is an very large, angry star. You can see the irregularity in the star's corona, where it is losing massive amounts of gas. Scientist have yet to explain why this is happening. This is the first time they have mapped and imaged a star other than the Sun.

Azure Dragon - 苍龙 - Han Dynasty 206 BCE-220 CE
The above stone was unearthed at Nanyang, Henan Province and depicts the 16 stars of the Azure or Green Dragon constellationn. It is a very ancient star chart. There seem to be two different versions of the Azure Dragon. Some face Virgo and some face away from Virgo, as this one does.

Figure 4 Stellarium images courtesy of Stellarium Developers, Copyright © 2000-2016 Photo © 2004 Marilyn Shea, Ph.D., Professor of Psychology, University of Maine at Farmington, used by permission.

Here, I have diagramed where the stars on the ancient stone chart are in relationship to one another and found the exact stars in the sky. Measurements are not exact, but overall, they are very, very close. There may be some distortion from the computer model simulating a curved sky. Next, I made a "ghost" of the stone image and overplayed it onto the stars.

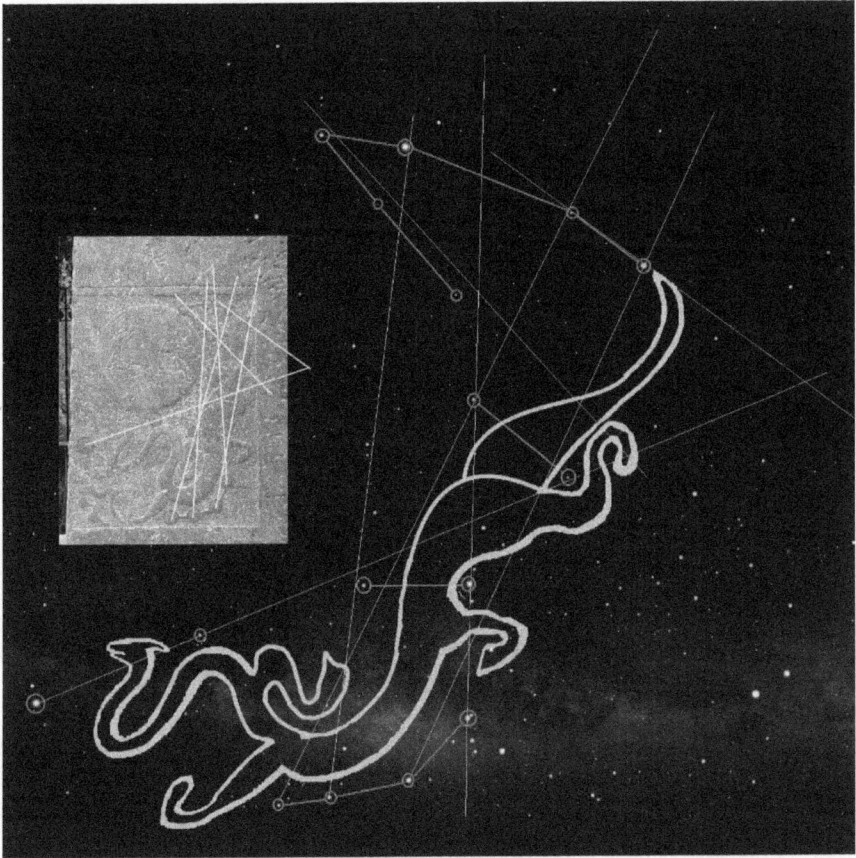

Figure 5 Stellarium images courtesy of Stellarium Developers, Copyright ©
2000-2016. Photo © 2004 Marilyn Shea, Ph.D., Professor of Psychology,
University of Maine at Farmington, used by permission.

Here, the distortion is easy to see. One thing
I've noticed in both versions of the Azure Dragon, (Or
for our purposes, "The Great Red Dragon"), is the four
stars at the bottom form a curve, echo the four stars
which form a curve at the top (including the stars
Spica, Heze 79 Vir, Arcturus and Izar 36 Boo) This
arrangement makes it easy to accidentally reverse the
orientation of the dragon, making the head the tail
and vise versa.

If you were to plot the other constellations onto this chart, it would be clear that the asterisms making up the Azure Dragon have changed over thousands of years. If you compare figure 5 with figure 2, you'll see that the older version faces away from Virgo. (The thought occurs to me that the Milky Way represented a river, or possibly "death", and may play a large role in the metaphoric movement of planets. The Dragon depicted coming into or out of the river (death or Hell) could have great significance as it relates to the Great Red Dragon (Satan).

In works of art showing Chinese Dragons, it's not unusual to show the dragon holding an orb known as Yeouiju, said to give its owner omnipotence.

Here, I would like to point out that the Historic Chinese National Flag, which features the Azure Dragon, has it looking toward an orb. It is my belief, based on the position of the dragon constellation in the stars, that the red rob represents the star "Arcturus". It may be interesting to note that the dragon does not seem to be going after Jupiter. But this would be consistent with scripture, when Satan tried to kill the baby Jesus, by having King Herod kill all the babies in the area. Jesus escaped with Mary and Joseph to Egypt, thus the Dragon went after the wrong star. Also, Arcturus is always there, in front of the Dragon, whereas, Jupiter only passes through.

The Azure Dragon on the national flag of China during the Qing dynasty, 1889-1912. Note the similarity to the rubbing collected by D.C. Graham above.

China Daily reports:

"Qinglong town, or "Azure Dragon Town", 10 kilometers north of Taiyuan in Shanxi, used to be a village surrounded by sweet wormwoods sitting at the main road connecting Shanxi province, a historical economic powerhouse, with Inner Mongolia, since early Qing Dynasty (1644-1911)"

As an aside, I did take note of the reference to "wormwoods", a term used in Revelation 8:10 "The third angel sounded his trumpet, and a great star, blazing like a torch, fell from the sky on a third of the rivers and on the springs of water— 11 the name of the star is Wormwood.[a] A third of the waters turned bitter, and many people died from the waters that had become bitter."

The herb "wormwood" is a bitter tasting shrub that grows up to about four feet tall. It is used for different types of beverages, medicines and has been historically used to wean babies (because of its bitter taste).

More details on the Azure Dragon
"an enormous red dragon with seven heads and ten horns and seven crowns on its heads."

The Scripture calls this constellation the "Great Red Dragon", and there is a good reason for that. First, the Chinese developed their own name for the dragon. Secondly, the "heart of the dragon" is the well known star Antares, which is a red star and appears red in comparison to other stars in the sky. I believe this is why the scripture calls it "The Great Red Dragon". Also, if you count the most prominent stars near the head of Scorpio and the main part of Libra, you may interpret seven "heads" on this red dragon. I believe the ten horns and seven crowns is more figuratively referring to the layer of the story that takes place on the Earth, involving kings and countries.

Chapter 6

The Leonids

Revelation 12:3-4

"Then another sign appeared in heaven: an enormous red dragon with seven heads and ten horns and seven crowns on its heads. Its tail swept a third of the stars out of the sky and flung them to the earth."

So, while I was studying and praying about the stars, the Lord revealed to me a cycle that happens each year. Draco, the dragon constellation that circles the North Star, most likely represents part of the prophecy in Revelation 12. As Draco proceeds tail first around the North Star, he sweeps 1/3 of the stars of the sky with his tail. After one complete revolution, which takes a year, the Leonids (as well as other meteor showers) "casts" those stars symbolically to the earth. This represents Christ (Leo, the Lion of Judah) casting Satan and his angels to the Earth.

In support of my theory about Draco, in my research I ran across this quote from Proctor,

"One might almost, if fancifully disposed, recognize the gradual displacement of the Dragon from his old place of honor, in certain traditions of the downfall of the great Dragon whose, 'tale drew the third part of the stars of heaven, ' alluded to in the Revelation 12:4 and the conclusion of that verse, 'did cast them to the earth, ' would show a possible reference to meteors."

"English: The most famous depiction of the 1833 Leonid meteorite shower was actually produced in 1889 for the Adventist book Bible Readings for the Home Circle - the engraving is by Adolf Vollmy based upon an original painting by the Swiss artist Karl Jauslin, that is in turn based on a first-person account of the 1833 storm by a minister, Joseph Harvey Waggoner on his way from Florida to New Orleans."

I included the above illustration because I was fascinated to find out that during 1833, so many meteorites fell during the Leonid Meteor shower that estimates are as high as 100,000 meteorites blazed across the sky per hour! Witnesses said, it appeared that every star in the sky was falling to the earth and some even wondered if there were parts of the night sky that no longer contained stars. It was a cataclysmic event and every 33 years, there is the potential to have another one. The Leonid Meteor showers are caused by the Earth passing through the tail of the Tempel-Tuttle Comet. Estimates say the next really big Leonid meteor shower could be in 2031, however some believe Jupiter has caused the comet to pass in a different course, reducing the showers.

There are several meteor showers in both Leo and Virgo that preceeded the conception, involving Jupiter, the Sun and the Moon in 2016: The Leonids, Leonids minora, the Virginids and interestingly, a comet that will only pass one time traveled from Leo to Virgo, prior to the conception.

There are just so many details I have to skip over because there would not be room in an entire library for the information contained in the stars. You can even look up the Hebrew names of the stars and each constellation tells a story, spelling out sentences and messages. If you are interested in this kind of research, look up information on the deacon constellations of Virgo and be careful to look for information that acknowledges God. Stay away from the astrology and fortune telling. This is a topic can be researched and investigated literally for the rest of one's life. God's creation is magnificent, both vast and detailed.

Chapter 7

What does the Bible say about the Stars?

The Bible talks about the stars quite a bit. In this chapter, I would like to do what Jesus did with His Disciples. I want to take you through all the scriptures and explain what it says about a certain subject, in this case, the stars. There are some references left out, but I hope I have included all the pertinent ones. It's quite surprising to see just how much the Bible talks about the stars!

Words matter. Please pay special attention to each word, as you read what the Bible says about the stars. I add my commentary for the sake of teaching and to help the reader understand how these different passages have always tied into the bigger picture of Biblical prophecy. As you might recall, there are instances in the Bible where the prophets were told to "seal up the words" until the end times. We are now in those end times and these prophecies are intended for us and are now being revealed to us.

Let's examine the scriptures from the beginning and see what they have to reveal about the stars.

Genesis 1:14
And God said, "Let there be lights in the expanse of the sky to separate the day from the night, and let them serve as signs to mark the seasons and days and years, and let them be lights in the expanse of the sky to give light on the earth." And it was so. God made two great lights - the greater to govern the day and the lesser to govern the night.

He also made the stars. God set them in the expanse of the sky to give light on the earth, to govern the day and the night, and to separate light from darkness.

And God saw that it was good. And there was evening and there was morning - the fourth day."

So, VERY early on, God reveals His purpose for creating the stars. This early declaration is very significant in Hebrew literature and law. The older the law or principle, the more important it was. Newer laws or principles were overridden by older ones. This is why Jesus, when dealing with matters of the law, always refers back to the oldest possible text, overruling the religious philosophy of the day.

What is the purpose of the stars according to the above passage? Threefold: 1. to give light, simple enough, 2. to separate light and dark, day and night, and 3. "Let them be for signs, (comma)(separate thought - and) to mark the seasons and days and years". That last point is what I am most interested in. There are a few concepts that can be asserted from this statement. First, the sun, moon and stars serve as signs.

Secondly, those signs mark seasons, "days" (this could mean the Sun marking off days, or the moon marking off weeks or months) and years. The lights in the sky are a God-given calendar. They mark the year, they tell us what season it is as well as whether it is day or night and even what time of day or night it is. In one sense, it's like a chronographic watch, a time-piece, which indeed all of our timepieces are designed after. So, it's God who designed "time", years, seasons and set the sun, moon, stars and planets in place, regularly revolving and moving through space in a predictable way.

But is that all they are intended to do? Do these signs tell us more than just what time it is?

Do the prophecies about the stars also tell us what time we live in on the prophetic side of things? Let's see what else the Bible says about the stars.

Gen 37:9 - Joseph's Dreams

Then he had another dream, and he told it to his brothers. "Listen, "he said, "I had another dream, and this time the sun and moon and eleven stars were bowing down to me."

So, Joseph, one of 12 children born to Jacob (Israel) had a dream. In this dream there were some interesting details. The sun and moon represented Joseph's parents, Israel (Jacob) and Rachel. The 11 stars represented Joseph's 11 brothers. It is also interesting to note the number of stars. It would be a logical assumption that Joseph was also represented by a star in the dream, making a total of 12 stars. This is supported in part because in his previous dream, Joseph was represented by a bundle of grain which stood upright, while his brothers were represented by bundles that bowed down. We have already examined Rev. 12:1-2 where it mentions 12 stars. The Crown of 12 Stars in Revelation 12 is most likely the 12 Tribes of Israel, corresponding to the 12 sons of Jacob, (whose name was changed to Israel). Going back to Genesis and finding this comparison between Israel's 12 sons and stars gives a strong Biblical basis for concluding that the 12 star crown of Revelation 12 is valid.

I Kings "Mazzaloth" Reference

The Mazzaroth is mentioned in the Bible only one time in the Book of Job. A similar word is used one other time in the book of II Kings 23:4, referring to the worship of the stars. Mazzaroth is thought to refer to the 12 constellations along the sun's ecliptic, while "Mazzaloth" is considered to be the worship of the stars, similar to astrology. (Notice the similarity of the two words and how similar our words are for astronomy and astrology)

II Kings 23:4 The king ordered Hilkiah the high priest, the priests next in rank and the doorkeepers to remove from the temple of the Lord all the articles made for Baal and Asherah and all the starry hosts (Mazzaloth). He burned them outside Jerusalem in the fields of the Kidron Valley and took the ashes to Bethel.

Job 9:9

"He is the Maker of the Bear and Orion. Pleiades and the constellations of the south."

This verse tells us the constellations originated with God, He is the creator of the constellations. The Bear, refers to Ursula Major, a constellation which contains the asterism, or "easily recognizable group of stars" know as the Big Dipper. We will see later a reference to the Little Dipper, known as Ursula Minor. There is a footnote in Job 9 that says "The Bear could actually be Leo with Leo Minor. (The two "bear" some similarity!) Orion is a well known constellation, a prominent feature of which is Orion's Belt. Orion is thought to be an image of the conquering Messiah, Jesus.

Job 22:12 "Is not God in the heights of heaven? And see how lofty are the highest stars!

In Job, Eliphaz the Temanite implies that God resides beyond the highest stars. The 3rd Heaven.

Job 26:7
"He spreads out the northern skies over empty space; He suspends the earth over nothing."
        I included this verse, because it talks very accurately about space, the planets and it also presents scientifically correct information about planet earth being suspended in space, "over nothing". Often, people will be critical of poetic and figurative language used in the Bible, but here we see that in Job, the oldest book of the Bible, the idea of earth being suspended in space is accurately described before any other document, scientist or way of thinking even came close to this kind of scientifically accurate statement about the nature of planets and space.

Job 38:31-33a
31 "Can you bind the cluster of the Pleiades,
Or loose the belt of Orion?
32 Can you bring out Mazzaroth in its season?
Or can you guide the Great Bear with its cubs?
33 Do you know the ordinances of the heavens?

        It is significant to understand that the Jewish people had names for the constellations, as well as a term for the stations of the Sun as it passed through the constellations. They called this the "Mazzaroth", which is mentioned in Job 38:31-33

It was used in both good and bad ways by the Jewish people. Sometimes they turned from God and worshipped the Sun, Moon and Stars. Sometimes they used the story in the stars to teach their children about God, the Messiah, and the struggle between good and evil.

The above verses also mention Ursula Major and Ursula Minor, "the Great Bear with its cubs". Some may note that today, Ursula Major only has one cub. This is most likely due to the renaming of minor constellations over the millennia. There are several smaller constellations surrounding Ursula Major that could easily be interpreted to be her cubs, such as Canes Venatici, Leo Minor and several others.

There is so much information about the stars and constellations contained in this brief passage! First, it mentions the Pleiades, a tight cluster of stars in the constellation Taurus (the bull), which is referred to as beautiful or twinkling. Next it asks, "Can you loose the cords of Orion?", referring to Orion's belt, a bright set of three stars in a line.

According to research by Christian Author J. Warner Wallace, the Pleiades are a group of stars that are bound together by gravitational attraction, while the stars of Orion are moving apart, just as the scripture foretold.

In Job 38 we also see a reference to constellations being visible in relation to different seasons, just as Genesis says is one of the purposes for which God created the stars. In Hebrew translations, "constellations in their seasons" is called the "Mazzaroth", the name in Hebrew of the Zodiac's 12 main constellations (Zodiac means stages of the sun's path through the constellations in 12 months).

After that it mentions "the Bear with its cubs". The bear would refer to Ursula Major and cubs to Ursula Minor (and perhaps other constellations nearby which earlier could have been interpreted as cubs such as Canes Venatici, Leo Minor or segments of the Lynx). (again, the Bear with its cubs could also be Leo and Leo minor)

The question, "Do you know the laws of the Heavens?" is an interesting one, because it was largely the study of the stars, and the movement of the sun, moon and planets that led to the development of complex math, such as trigonometry and many other sciences, in order to calculate and predict future placements of the heavenly bodies. While man is still grasping to understand the laws God set in place which governs the heavens, it is by studying these observable forces that much of what we call "science" came to be. Principles such as gravity or the speed of light have been observed at work in God's creation and form the basis for scientific laws.

Psalm 19:1-6
"The heavens declare the glory of God, the skies proclaim the work of his hands. Day after day they pour forth speech; night after night they display knowledge. There is no speech or language where their voice is not heard. Their voice goes out into all the earth, their words to the ends of the world. In the heavens he has pitched a tent for the sun, which is like a bridegroom coming forth from his pavilion, like a champion rejoicing to run his course. It rises at one end of the heavens and makes its circuit to the other; nothing is hidden from its heat."

I just can't emphasize the importance of this passage enough when it comes to the original meaning and purpose of the stars. God made them! They are the works of His hands, not the result of imaginative people. What does it mean, "Day after day they pour forth speech; night after night they display knowledge"? It means that God intended His stars to tell a story that glorifies Him! God is also faithful to tell every person on the face of the Earth the story of redemption. The fact that "there is no speech or language where their voice is not heard" is powerful! The constellations cross both language and culture barriers and carry a powerful message in the form of pictures, symbols and metaphors. Only the God who created the Universe could position stars, light-years apart, bigger and smaller, to tell a story in the sky. It's not just a "Christianization" of the stars and constellations. Whether Greek, Babylonian or Egyptian, many of the constellations carried the same meaning. Virgo is a woman and usually a virgin who, not-so-coincidentally is associated with fertility, Immaculate Conception and virgin birth. The way the Sun, Moon and planets pass through the 12 constellations and tell that story over and over, adding meaning and timing like a great clock... I am over-awed at His the works of God's hands!

Amos 5:8
He who made the Pleiades and Orion,
    who turns midnight into dawn
    and darkens day into night,
who calls for the waters of the sea
    and pours them out over the face of the land—
    the Lord is his name.

The prophet Amos sounds a lot like the book of Job here, as does King David in the Psalms, when talking about the stars. They glorify God and draw attention to His mighty power.

Isaiah 40:26
Lift your eyes and look to the heavens; who created all these? He who brings out the starry host one by one, and calls them each by name. Because of his great power and mighty strength, not one of them is missing.

Here we see a declaration! God is the one who created the stars. He names them. In the Bible names had a lot of meaning. A name was almost like a destiny, or a description of what that person would be like. The stars are God's. They are for His glory.

Isaiah 7:14
Therefore the Lord himself will give you a sign: The virgin will be with child and will give birth to a son, and will call him Immanuel (God with us).

This is a significant prophecy concerning the birth of Jesus, given hundreds of years before His birth. It speaks of 1. The origin of the sign is from God, 2. There will be a virgin, 3. She will have an Immaculate Conception, 4. She will give birth to a son, 5. The son will be called "God with us". All of these things were fulfilled by Jesus Christ.

Isaiah 9:1b-2, 9:6-7   The Sign of Immanuel

"in the future he will honor Galilee of the Gentiles, by the way of the sea, along the Jordan - The people walking in darkness have seen a great light; on those living in the land of the shadow of death a light has dawned...

For to us a child is born, to us a son is given, and the government will be on his shoulders. And he will be called Wonderful Counselor, Mighty God, Everlasting Father, Prince of Peace.

Of the increase of his government and peace there will be no end. He will reign on David's throne and over his kingdom, establishing and upholding it with justice and righteousness from that time on and forever. The zeal of the Lord Almighty will accomplish this."

I could write a book on this passage alone. It tells us where the Messiah (Jesus) was going to be born, that He would be the light of the world, that He would be born of the Kingly line of Israel, and it speaks very clearly of His deity, that He would be God in the flesh.

Isaiah 13:9-10
"See, the day of the Lord is coming - a cruel day, with wrath and fierce anger - to make the land desolate and destroy the sinners within it. The stars of heaven and their constellations will not show their light. The rising sun will be darkened and the moon will not give it's light... Therefore I will make the heavens tremble; and the earth will shake from its place at the wrath of the Lord Almighty, in the day of his burning anger."

I believe this passage talks mainly about "Great and Terrible Day of The Lord", the ultimate destruction and re-creation of Heaven and Earth. It's significant to note that the constellations will not give their light. This seems to set this passage apart. It is not simply one of the blood moons or an eclipse. The very heavens will tremble and the earth will shake from its place!

Joel 2:30-32
"I will show wonders in the heavens and on the earth, blood and fire and billows of smoke. The sun will be turned to darkness and the moon to blood BEFORE the coming of the great and dreadful day of the LORD. And everyone who calls on the name of the LORD will be saved."

The prophet Joel spoke these very familiar words to tell us ahead of time what would happen BEFORE the coming of the great and dreadful (terrible) day of the LORD. We have seen these kinds of signs in the heavens very recently! The four blood moons, separated by a solar eclipse (visible from Israel), as well as the Great American Eclipse (visible in the USA) seem to be telling both Jews and Christians, "The time is near!"

The word for "heavens" here, originally written in Hebrew, was quoted by Peter in Acts 2:19-20 in Greek. In Greek "ourano", the word from which we get the name Uranus, is defined by Strong's Concordance as "the sky, the heaven, a) the visible heavens: the atmosphere, the sky the starry heavens, b)the spiritual heavens.

In Hebrew, the word Peter uses, is also used in Genesis to describe where God put the Sun, Moon and stars, as well as when it says, "Then God said, Let us make man in our own image, in our likeness, and let them rule over the fish of the sea and the birds of the air." That last part where is says, "of the air" (of heaven), is the word, "hassamayim".

Micah 5:2-3

But you, Bethlehem Ephratha, though you are small among the clans of Judah, out of you will come for me one who will be ruler over Israel, whose origins are from of old, from ancient times (from days of eternity) Therefore Israel will be abandoned until the time when she who is in labor gives birth and the rest of his brothers return to join the Israelites.

Here we see a prophetic birth announcement! The Messiah will come from Bethlehem. This is the passage the chief priests and teachers of the law turned to, when asked where the Messiah would be born. Interestingly, "until the time when she who is in labor gives birth" could easily fit into the narritive of the constellation Virgo (the virgin) as we see described in Rev. 12. Also, the phrase "and the rest of his brothers return to join the Israelites" is interesting because the stars in the constellation Leo are supposed to represent the sons of Israel, however there are only 9 stars! This is explained in picture form for us by the history of Israel found in the Bible. In Numbers chapter 33, the tribes of Gad, Reuben and the half tribe of Manasseh stay on the East side of the Jordan. These tribes are represented by the three wandering stars Venus, Mercury and Mars which join the constellation Leo in Revelation 12 to form a "crown of 12 stars at the head of the virgin". Also, Judah is ruling over them, because the 9 stars of Leo (9 western tribes) are in the constellation representing Judah, the Lion, and the other 3 (3 eastern tribes) are Judah's scepter. So, we can see how Israel continues to be a picture for us of the prophecies concerning the stars.

Matthew 24:30 The sign of the Son of Man
"How shall these things be, since I am a virgin?"
The Holy Spirit will come upon you and the power of
the Most High will overshadow you, and so the holy
one to be born will be called, "The Son of God".

For commentary on this verse, please refer to Chapter
4 "The Virgin"

Luke 21:25-28
**25 And there shall be signs in the sun, and in
the moon, and in the stars; and upon the earth
distress of nations, with perplexity; the sea and
the waves roaring;   26 Men's hearts failing them
for fear, and for looking after those things which
are coming on the earth: for the powers of
heaven shall be shaken.   27 And then shall they
see the Son of man coming in a cloud with power
and great glory.   28 And when these things
begin to come to pass, then look up, and lift up
your heads; for your redemption draweth nigh.**

Luke 21 clearly confirms what all the other
passages about signs in the Sun, Moon and Stars are
saying.   We are witnessing the signs that were
foretold to happen just before the return of Jesus
Christ "in a cloud".   I believe this is referring to the
Rapture, because He comes in a cloud, but it does not
say He comes down to the ground.   I put these two
passages in bold, because they are very significant.

Acts 2:19-20, "I will show wonders in the heavens (the sky, same word as Rev 12) above and signs on the earth below, blood and fire and billows of smoke. The sun will be turned to darkness and the moon to blood before the coming of the great and glorious day of the Lord." (Paul, quoting from Joel 2:28-32)

It's interesting to note that Paul is interpreting Joel's word "dreadful" as "glorious", perhaps the words used are similar to how the word "awful" has a negative connotation, but originally meant "full of awe".

Words are important because they help us know the difference between one thing and another. We need to understand "The Day of The Lord" is associated with the Second Coming of Jesus Christ to the earth. However, He does not come to the earth when we are ruptured. At the rapture, He comes in the clouds, we are caught up together with Him and return to the third heaven, where God's throne is. When Jesus returns to the earth, He will bring us with Him and destroy all of His enemies, followed by the setting up of His Kingdom here on the earth for 1000 years, known as the Millennium, or the Millennial reign of Christ, also called "Entering into His rest". A Sabbath or seventh day for all the earth to give both us and the earth a rest from all labor.

1 Thess. 5:3
For when they shall say, Peace and safety; then sudden destruction cometh upon them, as travail upon a woman with child; and they shall not escape.

I deal with this verse in the chapter on "The Virgin".

2 Thessalonians 2 The Man of Lawlessness
2:2 Concerning the coming of our Lord Jesus Christ and our being gathered to him, we ask you, brothers and sisters, 2 not to become easily unsettled or alarmed by the teaching allegedly from us—whether by a prophecy or by word of mouth or by letter—asserting that the day of the Lord has already come.
3 Don't let anyone deceive you in any way, for that day will not come until the rebellion occurs and the man of lawlessness[a] is revealed, the man doomed to destruction. 4 He will oppose and will exalt himself over everything that is called God or is worshiped, so that he sets himself up in God's temple, proclaiming himself to be God.

I wanted to include this passage because it deals directly with the end times and gives us things to watch for. It specifically tells us that we will be "gathered to Christ" (Ruptured) ONLY after the Anti-Christ is revealed, and sets himself up in God's temple, proclaiming himself to be God. So again, when the Temple starts to be rebuilt, we know the time is very short!

Revelation 6:12 I watched as he opened the sixth seal. The sun turned black like sackcloth made of goat hair, the whole moon turned blood red, and the stars in the sky fell to earth, as late figs drop from a tree when shaken by a strong wind. The sky receded like a scroll, rolling up, and every mountain and island was removed from its place.
This is a tough one to comment on. The Sun does turn black when there is a full solar eclipse, as we shall see on August 21st, 2017 (as I edit this, I just got back from the eclipse this week and I am sitting here wearing the t-shirt!).

However, the moon turning blood red, implies that it is not the Moon that is eclipsing the Sun. Some have argued for another "planet" eclipsing the sun (which no planets pass between the Earth and the Sun in a way that would cause an eclipse), so some have postulated that there is a "rogue planet" they've dubbed "Niburu". There is only sketchy, unverifiable evidence for this and NASA says "It doesn't exist". NASA tracks all near-Earth objects and keeps a detailed catalog of anything that could potentially impact or come near the Earth. I usually conclude that the person talking about Niburu is a conspiracy theorist, because they have to completely ignore NASA and every credible astronomer, the world over, to believe in it. It also does not reflect well on those of us who take the Bible seriously. The Bible makes no mention of this mythical planet, only "a mountain that falls in the sea" (mountains are much smaller than planets and would therefore be considered an asteroid, comet or meteor) and "Wormwood", which is mentioned in much the same way.

And here is the final word, the End Times foretold by Jesus Himself:

Mark 13
The Destruction of the Temple and Signs of the End Times
1 As Jesus was leaving the temple, one of his disciples said to him, "Look, Teacher! What massive stones! What magnificent buildings!"
2 "Do you see all these great buildings?" replied Jesus. "Not one stone here will be left on another; every one will be thrown down."
3 As Jesus was sitting on the Mount of Olives opposite the temple, Peter, James, John and Andrew asked him privately, 4 "Tell us, when will these things happen? And what will be the sign that they are all about to be fulfilled?"
5 Jesus said to them: "Watch out that no one deceives you. 6 Many will come in my name, claiming, 'I am he,' and will deceive many. 7 When you hear of wars and rumors of wars, do not be alarmed. Such things must happen, but the end is still to come. 8 Nation will rise against nation, and kingdom against kingdom. There will be earthquakes in various places, and famines. These are the beginning of birth pains.
9 "You must be on your guard. You will be handed over to the local councils and flogged in the synagogues. On account of me you will stand before governors and kings as witnesses to them. 10 And the gospel must first be preached to all nations. 11 Whenever you are arrested and brought to trial, do not worry beforehand about what to say. Just say whatever is given you at the time, for it is not you speaking, but the Holy Spirit.

12 "Brother will betray brother to death, and a father his child. Children will rebel against their parents and have them put to death. 13 Everyone will hate you because of me, but the one who stands firm to the end will be saved.

14 "When you see 'the abomination that causes desolation'[a] standing where it[b] does not belong— let the reader understand—then let those who are in Judea flee to the mountains. 15 Let no one on the housetop go down or enter the house to take anything out. 16 Let no one in the field go back to get their cloak. 17 How dreadful it will be in those days for pregnant women and nursing mothers! 18 Pray that this will not take place in winter, 19 because those will be days of distress unequaled from the beginning, when God created the world, until now—and never to be equaled again.

20 "If the Lord had not cut short those days, no one would survive. But for the sake of the elect, whom he has chosen, he has shortened them. 21 At that time if anyone says to you, 'Look, here is the Messiah!' or, 'Look, there he is!' do not believe it. 22 For false messiahs and false prophets will appear and perform signs and wonders to deceive, if possible, even the elect. 23 So be on your guard; I have told you everything ahead of time.

24 "But in those days, following that distress,

"'the sun will be darkened,
    and the moon will not give its light;
25 the stars will fall from the sky,
    and the heavenly bodies will be shaken.'[c]

26 "At that time people will see the Son of Man coming in clouds with great power and glory. 27 And he will send his angels and gather his elect from the four winds, from the ends of the earth to the ends of the heavens.

28 "Now learn this lesson from the fig tree: As soon as its twigs get tender and its leaves come out, you know that summer is near. 29 Even so, when you see these things happening, you know that it[d] is near, right at the door. 30 Truly I tell you, this generation will certainly not pass away until all these things have happened. 31 Heaven and earth will pass away, but my words will never pass away.

The Day and Hour Unknown

32 "But about that day or hour no one knows, not even the angels in heaven, nor the Son, but only the Father. 33 Be on guard! Be alert[e]! You do not know when that time will come. 34 It's like a man going away: He leaves his house and puts his servants in charge, each with their assigned task, and tells the one at the door to keep watch.

35 "Therefore keep watch because you do not know when the owner of the house will come back—whether in the evening, or at midnight, or when the rooster crows, or at dawn. 36 If he comes suddenly, do not let him find you sleeping. 37 What I say to you, I say to everyone: 'Watch!'"

Notes - Recent News & Discoveries by other people

I wanted to be thorough and list a few discoveries that other people have made. Some of these discoveries are not specifically mentioned in the prophecy of Revelation 12, or in the Bible, so I have not focused on them, for lack of Biblical basis. Others, like the Feast of Trumpets are very Biblically based, but I did not discover them. I've included this information because I don't want my readers to be unaware of them, as some of them are quite significant.

There is a lot of information out there on the Jewish feasts and particularly the "Feast of Trumpets" and Jewish New Year, called Rosh Hashanah. The Bible does tell us that we will be caught up "at the last trumpet" and that the Lord will return with the loud sounding of a trumpet. I also find it quite fascinating that we are in Jewish year 5777. There is an understanding that comes from 2 Peter 3 that says "With the Lord a day is like a thousand years, and a thousand years are like a day." This verse, coupled with many others leads some to believe that the Earth's history will last a total of 7 thousand years, in correspondence to the 7 days of creation. On the 7th day God rested. During the 7th Millennium and the Millennial Reign of Christ we will "enter into His rest". Also, the number 7 in scripture is considered to be the "number of completion" and to see it 3 times in the year 5777 is significant.

It's all a picture for us to understand. Here is some information I found that summarizes research by a few other people.

from Wikipedia:

"The Revelation 12 Sign may coincide with the High Holy Day of Rosh Hashanah on the Jewish calendar, which is also called the Feast of Trumpets. The Feast of Trumpets is the first of the Fall Feasts and its timing is traditionally based on the visibility of the new moon, which in 2017 is expected to either begin on the evening of September 21st and end on the evening of the 22nd (if the 2% illuminated moon is sighted) or begin on the evening of the 22nd and end on the evening of the 23rd when the sign is fulfilled. Rosh Hashanah is the Jewish New Year celebration, in this case marking the end of the year 5777 (sometimes abbreviated to the significant number 777) and the beginning of 5778. The Feast of Trumpets in Jewish tradition is believed to be a day when the dead will be resurrected and judgement will begin while Christians believe the period describes the tribulation period found in the Book of Revelation.

It has also been pointed out by Revelation 12 Sign proponents that a number of eminent biblical scholars support their particular interpretation of Revelation 12, including John Nelson Darby, Harry Ironside, and more recently Dr. Michael Svigel.

The apocalyptic symbol of a woman in labor is found throughout Jewish and Christian Scriptures, which proponents suggest is evidence of the September 2017 alignment's importance in prophecy. These particular Scriptures include Isaiah 13:6-13[16], Isaiah 26:17-21[17], Isaiah 66:7-11[18], Jeremiah 30:4-11[19], Jeremiah 49:23-27[20], Micah 5:3[21], Matthew 24:8[22], Mark 13:8[23], and 1 Thessalonians 5:3.[24]"

Here is a link to the article. It also lists several organizations and researchers who have corroborated the Sign mentioned in Revelation 12 being visible in the stars.

Some Perspective from Jewish Traditions

People will ascribe profound personal meaning to some of the craziest things, so that being said, there are many, many sites online that have a lot of speculation and baseless conclusions. Particularly those that are not scholarly and are only based on feelings or hunches. However, I found the following post (among many other "less interesting" comments) on

"Posted by "Anonymous"

Shabbat Shuvah ("Sabbath [of] Return" שבת שובה) refers to the Shabbat that occurs during the Ten Days of Repentance between Rosh Hashanah and Yom Kippur. Only one Shabbat can occur between these dates. This Shabbat is named after the first word of the Haftarah (Hosea 14:2-10) and literally means "Return!" It is perhaps a play on, but not to be confused with, the word Teshuvah (the word for repentance). Shabbat Shuva begins at sundown on Fri, 22 September 2017.

The Torah reading for this Shabbat, September 23, 2017, is only one chapter, but what a chapter it is! It is Deuteronomy chapter 32:1-52.

This special Torah reading is an amazing confirmation of the details we find in Revelation chapter 12. (There is no word for coincidence in the Hebrew language)

The very first verse of our Torah reading should get our attention...."Give ear O' heavens and let Me speak, and let the earth hear the words of My mouth" (Deuteronomy 32:1)

And the first scripture in Revelation 12 begins with these words, " And a great sign appeared in heaven"...the Greek word for "great" is "mega" which is translated as "loud" throughout the NT. So, the Lord is telling us from the very beginning of these two chapters that He is speaking loudly (mega) from the heavens and the earth needs to listen

We learn from Revelation 12 that the dragon/devil/Satan is going to be "thrown down to the earth and his angels (are) thrown down with him." (Rev.12:9) The dragon has arrived! And what do we read in our Torah scriptures for this day?...."new gods who have recently arrived." And these chilling words, "you sacrificed to demons and to (new) gods whom you have not known." (Deuteronomy 32:17)

We then learn in Revelation 12 that the Lord is going to carry His people to safety on the "two wings of the great eagle." (Revelation 12:14) And what do we read in our Torah scriptures for this day?..."Like an eagle...He spread His wings and caught them, and carried them on His wings" (Deuteronomy 32:11)

This is the Jubilee Year for Jerusalem (1967/2017)...and many believe this is a Jubilee Year on God's calendar as well (Abib 1, 2017) to (Adar 29, 2018).

I believe God gives us His answer whether or not it is Jubilee from our Torah scripture for this day, September 23, 2017. We read, "And He will atone for His land and for His people." (Deut.32:43) The word "atone" means He will "redeem" the land. And what does God say concerning Jubilee?...."For every piece of property you are to provide for the redemption of the land." (Leviticus 25:23)

And this is not all....there is much more! Give ear O' earth and hear the Words of His mouth!

Bendiciones!

[signed] Redroksaz"

C/2017 E1 Borisov

A comet named C/2017 E1 Borisov passed from Leo to Virgo. Some are hailing it as a metaphorical picture of the Immaculate Conception. In essence, Jupiter would be the "Seed of the Woman" and the comet would be the "Seed of God", to leave the origin of the baby Jesus unambiguous. Louis B. Vega (great star name by the way) covers the idea of the comet in the following essay. (I'm adding a disclaimer here. I do not agree with many of Louis Vega's ideas. This is an interesting event but it is not mentioned in Revelation 12, or anywhere else in the Bible and I believe my explanation of the Immaculate Conception in Chapter 4 most certainly IS in the Bible and therefore supported Biblically. However, Louis Vega does a good job covering this comet and relating it to the life of Jesus.)

The following link leads to Louis B. Vega's article titled, "REVELATION 12 SIGN CONCEPTION COMET, C/2017 E1, The Impregnation of the Virgin"

http://nebula.wsimg.com/2fd138747ae34e1a9c 4432881b5d94f2?AccessKeyId=D40106E1331C2 4ABD7C3&disposition=0&alloworigin=1

The Planet "Niburu"

I find this theory to be completely without merit. There is absolutely no scientific evidence supporting the idea of a rogue planet or dwarf star hurtling towards Earth, or Jupiter. If there were, the science, astronomy and space agencies worldwide would be confirming it. So, sorry Niburu fans... "Niburu" is a conspiracy theory.

Special note
8-8-17

After having discovered the crown of 12 stars on my own, not having seen it before anywhere at all, and having written about it for more than a year, I found a man named Patrick Archbold, who like myself had come to this conclusion: "And upon her head we find a crown of twelve stars, formed by the usual nine stars of the constellation Leo with the addition of the planets Mercury, Venus, and Mars."
http://remnantnewspaper.com/web/index.php/articles/item/2127-apocalypse-now-another-great-sign-rises-in-the-heavens
I take this as confirmation that I am on the right track.

Famous Quotes:
"As I read the news, I can't help but wonder if we are in the last hours before our Lord Jesus Christ returns to rescue His church..." - Franklin Graham, President and CEO of the Billy Graham Evangelistic Association, amd Samaritan's Purse

"Dear Lord Jesus, I know that I am a sinner, and I ask for Your forgiveness. I believe You died for my sins and rose from the dead. I turn from my sins and invite You to come into my heart and life." - Billy Graham, evangelist.

(For more information on how to become a Christian, visit:
http://www.davidjeremiah.org/site/about/becoming_a_christian.aspx) Or find a Bible believing church near you.

2 Peter 3:8-14

8 "But do not forget this one thing, dear friends: With the Lord a day is like a thousand years, and a thousand years are like a day. 9 The Lord is not slow in keeping his promise, as some understand slowness. Instead he is patient with you, not wanting anyone to perish, but everyone to come to repentance.
10 But the day of the Lord will come like a thief. The heavens will disappear with a roar; the elements will be destroyed by fire, and the earth and everything done in it will be laid bare.[a]
11 Since everything will be destroyed in this way, what kind of people ought you to be? You ought to live holy and godly lives 12 as you look forward to the day of God and speed its coming.[b] That day will bring about the destruction of the heavens by fire, and the elements will melt in the heat. 13 But in keeping with his promise we are looking forward to a new heaven and a new earth, where righteousness dwells.
14 So then, dear friends, since you are looking forward to this, make every effort to be found spotless, blameless and at peace with him."

Post Inscription:
(From one of the most poetic chapters in all the Bible)

Proverbs 12
"Of making many books there is no end,
and much study wearies the body.
Now all has been heard;
here is the conclusion of the matter:
Fear God and keep his commandments,
for this is the duty of all mankind.
For God will bring every deed into judgment,
including every hidden thing,
whether it is good or evil."

David M. Willhite lives in Oregon surrounded by nature, where he earns a living as a professional potter. His interests include art, songwriting, gardening and hosting an annual Art & Chocolate Festival, which he started in 2005. His past times include skim boarding, owning a chocolate shop, working in a laboratory and hosting his own daily radio show on Christian radio for over 6 years.
He has a cat named Mercury.
Fun Fact:
He has built several igloos and has slept the night in one!

Write to the author at

David Willhite
106 NW F St. #259
Grants Pass, OR 97526
or at
davidwillhite@hotmail.com

www.ingramcontent.com/pod-product-compliance
Lightning Source LLC
Chambersburg PA
CBHW021203020426
42331CB00003B/190